Denman

The Educational Heart of the WI

Val Horsler

Denman

The Educational Heart of the WI

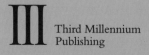
Third Millennium
Publishing

Denman has always held a special place in the heart of the WI. Since its foundation in 1948, WI members have enjoyed learning new skills and pursuing interests and hobbies with their fellow members. Along the way, new friendships have been forged, new careers started and horizons broadened.

When Lady Elizabeth Brunner proposed at the 1945 AGM that the WI should have its own college, she concluded 'What we teach must be related to the everyday practical things that make up our members' lives. In addition, there must be inspiration and a vision of wider horizons, so that life and the living of it becomes more important and worthwhile.' How many members would have believed that seventy years after it opened Denman would still be a centre for excellence and learning unrivalled in today's busy world?

In the early days, students shared a dormitory, took turns in making early morning tea, made their own beds and even helped prepare meals. Courses on offer have naturally changed over the years. As part of post-war austerity, members enjoyed general Country Housewives courses, which included cooking, gardening, preserving, household management and repairs and laundry so that they could return to their families better equipped to run their homes. Denman in the twenty-first century is more likely to include courses like silver clay jewellery, digital photography or world street food. The more traditional skills still flourish, however, and the WI Craft and Cookery Schools provide the backbone of the programme of courses. Present-day students now experience beautiful en suite accommodation, their own personal tea and coffee-making facilities and delicious food served at their tables.

Times may have changed but the ethos of Denman remains. Today Denman is a haven away from the hustle and bustle of modern life for members and non-members alike, ensuring that the magic of Denman is spread beyond WI membership. Denman has a strong following of members who return time and again, but also a high proportion of 'first timers' and it's a joy to see these newcomers discovering the Denman experience.

As Lady Brunner's vision moves into its eighth decade this wonderful book tells the story of Denman in pictures and celebrates its Platinum Anniversary – seventy years of learning and laughter.

We hope that it will encourage you to visit soon – you can be sure of a warm WI welcome.

Foreword

by Lynne Stubbings, NFWI Chair
and Pat Tulip, NFWI Vice Chair & Chair
NFWI Denman Committee

DENMAN GOVERNANCE

Denman is a wholly owned arm of the National Federation of Women's Institutes, and is also a connected charity of the NFWI, though it operates its own Trust Deed. It is governed by the NFWI Board of Trustees, chaired by the NFWI Chair, which delegates its management to a committee into which the Head of Denman and the senior management team at Denman report. The Head of Denman reports to the NFWI General Secretary and is a member of the NFWI Senior Management team.

Previous page Staff and students hold patchwork bedspreads made for the College bedrooms by Women's Institute members, 1950s.

Above Members of Cumberland WI, on opening day, with the rug they made for the College incorporating the WI 'For Home and Country' badge.

A model of the future Denman College, made by secondary school children in Abingdon, at an exhibition in Norfolk, c.1948.

When Sir Richard Livingstone opened Denman College in 1947, he spoke of 'the spirit of imagination, of faith, of enterprise, of perseverance, of cooperation' that had brought the College into being. Its survival seventy years on is tribute to the women who have nurtured it, rescued it at times of crisis, supported it, learned at it, and ensured that its essential quality has been maintained.

And it is about women. That is Denman's unique selling point: specifically, in the early days, rural women – though its embrace now reaches out to towns and cities as well – and specifically, to some extent, older women, many of whom, in the early days, had not had the benefit of a wide education. It is overseen by women, managed by women, staffed and attended by women. There are men too – there have been two male Principals – but they are vastly outnumbered.

Denman is both owned and managed by a voluntary organisation, the Women's Institute. Its roots drive deep into the WI's passion for the betterment of women, their education and their rightful position within their world. The WIs are hands-on too. Most of the rooms are in the care of one of the County Federations, which furnish and decorate them in accordance with their own local styles and crafts. The Federations and many of their constituent WIs give bursaries to enable women to attend the College who could not otherwise do so. It is a comfortable, friendly place within which to learn, and where it is easy to befriend and socialise with fellow WI members.

It is also unique as the only short-stay college for women, an environment of women with women learning together. It is testament to the vision of the founders, who wanted 'our place' to be a happy, warm, stimulating and welcoming environment where women could spread their wings. As so many of its alumnae attest, it is life-enhancing. That it still fulfils the initial mission of the women and men who were instrumental in its foundation is to be celebrated.

Introduction to Denman

Top (l–r) Lady Albemarle, Lady Denman, Betty Christmas and Sir Richard Livingstone approaching the College on opening day.

Bottom (l–r) Lady Brunner, Lady Denman and Sir Richard Livingstone on opening day.

To paraphrase and misquote Mary Tudor, the word 'education' is inscribed on the heart of the Women's Institute: 'When I am dead and opened you shall find Calais lying in my heart.'

It was the lack of domestic science education among countrywomen in Canada in the 1890s that led Adelaide Hoodless, after the death of her son through contaminated milk, to advocate the establishment of an institute for women which would promote scientific knowledge at home as well as at the workplace. For Edith Rigby, a militant suffragette who was a founding member of one of the first WIs in Lancashire, the establishment of a school for female mill workers in her home town, Preston, was a priority. Grace Hadow, academic, Fellow of Somerville College, Oxford, and later Principal of the college that was to become St Anne's, Oxford, was the first Vice-Chairman of the WI, provided the intellectual rigour underpinning its formidable founding principles, and wrote its first handbook. And these were just some of the powerful and determined women who saw the gaping hole in the lives of their compatriots and firmly believed that the establishment of the WI was the way to fill it.

They saw education as the means. The education of countrywomen was a fundamental part of the WI's first constitution in 1919, which defined it as providing 'a centre for educational and social intercourse and activities' and stated as one of its main objectives that it should 'make provision for the fuller education of countrywomen in citizenship, in public questions both national and international' and in agriculture, crafts, house-husbandry, health and cultural pursuits. This was just after the government had finally enfranchised women – though not yet on equal terms with men; this came within the next ten years, in 1928. As so many of the high-calibre women who headed the WI had themselves fought for female suffrage, they were determined that women should be prepared to take their proper places in public life.

Gertrude, Lady Denman, the first Chairman of the National Federation of Women's Institutes, wanted rural women to broaden their horizons, to take active roles in their communities, to free themselves from the constraints of rural duties, and to embrace a wider role both locally and nationally. On the broader educational stage, women's university colleges had been established for some fifty years in England and Wales, where women could study degree courses but initially without being admitted to degrees. London University was the pioneer in conferring degrees on women in 1878 and Oxford did so in 1920, though Cambridge hung on until a shamefully late 1948. But these opportunities were mainly open to upper- or middle-class urban women. Countrywomen were usually too bound up within the

A vision for education

Top left Lady Denman, 1933.

Top right Edith Rigby, 1900.

Bottom left Adelaide Hoodless, depicted on a Canadian stamp, c.1993.

Bottom right Grace Hadow, c.1919.

Adelaide Sophia Hoodless 1857-1910

FAMILY EDUCATOR · ÉDUCATRICE FAMILIALE

43 CANADA

LLANFAIRPWLL WOMENS' INSTITUTE, ANGLESEY. SEPT. 1915.
THE FIRST STARTED IN GREAT BRITAIN.

Above Britain's first WI, in Llanfairpwll, Anglesey.

Opposite left A Canadian quilt with a maple leaf design incorporating the WI's emblem, presented as a gift to Denman College, 1954.

Opposite right Llanfairpwll WI – the first WI meeting, 1915.

narrow limits of their busy lives to be able to dream of spreading their educational wings.

The WI had been an immediate success: in 1919, a mere four years after the first Institute was established in Anglesey in September 1915, there were 1,405 Institutes in England and Wales, and the momentum was building. Moreover, the thirst among the members for new experiences, more in-depth instruction, and wider opportunities for learning proved both surprising and challenging. As the educational programmes on offer at meetings expanded, there came a demand for full-blown, professionally taught courses. Local education authorities were called on to fulfil this need, and they rapidly found themselves overwhelmed by an unexpected new audience. The WI's focus on education also led to its growing involvement in educational planning at all levels of government; indeed, a Board of Education report in 1926 – by which time 3,328 Institutes had been established – commended the organisation for the success of its efforts which 'can only be regarded as phenomenal'. At the same time, the lack of proper practical education in agriculture for women was recognised, and Lady Denman was invited to chair a committee to address this issue. Her report, published in 1928, was prescient in recommending the establishment of a college for women specialising in that area.

The only immediate outcome of that report was the setting up of a network of Rural Domestic Economy instructresses, one of whom was later based at Denman; but nothing came then of the major recommendation, mainly because the 1930s were dominated by other concerns, notably the looming Second World War. However, the immediate post-war years saw a massive transformation in society overall, and in educational thinking in particular, and there was a ready audience for discussion of initiatives based on new and radical ideas. Lady Denman's 1928 proposal could now be revived through other agencies and in a different form.

DENMAN'S BEGINNINGS

When we are thinking about our own WI college, I want you to imagine a place that will be homely and welcoming, where in the pleasantest possible surroundings, away from the responsibilities and distractions of our usual lives, we can learn about useful practical crafts, and in addition where we can become better informed about the things going on in the world today, where we can learn more of our heritage, and consider and discuss our future.

These were the words of Elizabeth, Lady Brunner, speaking at the Women's Institutes' Annual General Meeting of 1945, when the idea of establishing the WI's own college was beginning to take widespread root. As she herself was later to say: 'When I first got to know the WI during the war, most of our members had left school at twelve, thirteen, or at the latest fourteen. In preparing for the Butler Act we were all absorbed in how to provide fuller, longer education … to provide skills for industry, training for the professions, but alongside a strong skein of history, literature, music, art, and crafts to widen horizons and develop gifts to achieve a complete individual …'

The seeds of this revived initiative had been sown in 1943 when Adeline Vernon, an Oxford graduate and a passionate advocate of education for women, was one of an energetic group of WI members who organised a conference at Radbrook College in Shrewsbury to discuss education and social security in post-war Britain. The other two prime movers were Elizabeth Christmas, then NFWI General Organiser and later to be Denman's first Warden, and Cicely McCall, Education Organiser. The main speaker was Sir Richard Livingstone, President of Corpus Christi College, Oxford, and an authority on adult education, whose speech was titled 'Education in a world adrift'. A strong advocate of education for women, he had been well briefed by his WI contacts; so, after vigorously criticising the British government for making no provision for adult education in its recent White Paper – later to form the basis of the 1944 Education Act (the Butler Act) – he asked his audience 'Why should not the Women's Institutes fill the gap? Why don't you start a people's college yourselves?' The motion was duly put to the conference and carried with great enthusiasm; to share the idea with WI members everywhere, Sir Richard contributed an article to *Home and Country* setting out the vision.

In the same issue, Cicely McCall wrote, 'Just an outsize dream? Not if we want it enough. Then it might become a thrilling possibility.' A letter from Margaret Turner from Limpsfield, Surrey, eloquently put the case from the grassroots:

Right Sir Richard Livingstone, President of Corpus Christi College, Oxford, cutting the ribbon on opening day.

Far right Sir Richard Livingstone giving a speech formally marking the opening of Denman College. Seated (l–r) are Gertrude Denman and Elizabeth Brunner.

Opposite Elizabeth Brunner, 1945.

Denman's beginnings

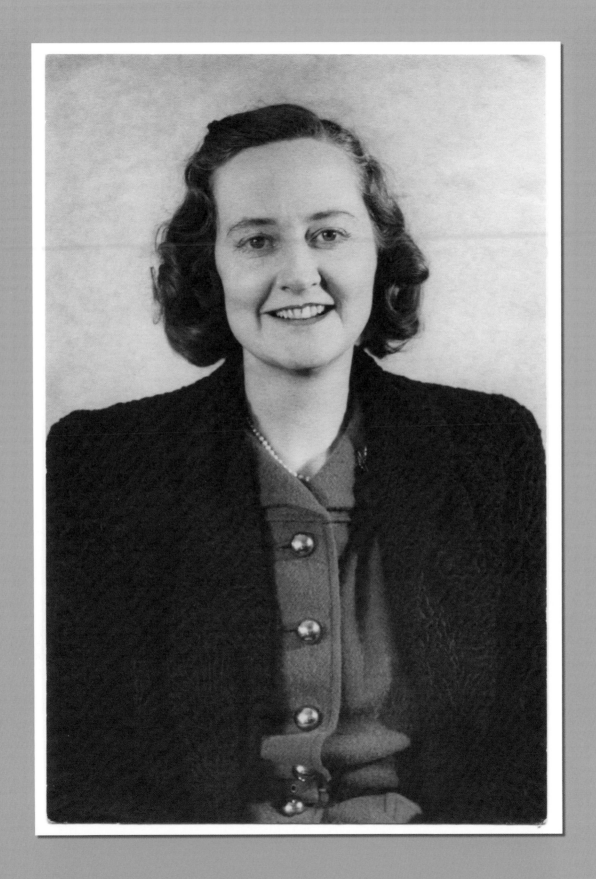

'I think the idea of "going to school", even if we go to school at our own WI college, will at first sound too dream-like to many members with heavy household responsibilities. On second thoughts, however, perhaps we can take heart … If, just for once in a lifetime, mother goes off for two days or even, giddy thought, for a week to mix with WI members whom she has never seen, and listen and discuss and talk her head off with them about bottling or schooling or housing or hospitals from morning to night … "going to school" for WI members will be something familiar and dear.'

The embryonic college was fortunate in having both Sir Richard Livingstone and Lady Brunner as its midwives. Along with many other passionate advocates of the idea, they shared a vision of a 'place of your own' where you came as a guest, but that would provide a focus and a framework for the broadening of horizons and the spreading of wings. Sir Richard saw the WI as a powerful force in the education of 'the Marthas as well as the Marys', valuing the potential of both, and he and Lady Brunner fully intended the college to be the centre of an educational force rippling outwards to communities all over the country.

The next step was to formalise the process by putting the idea as a resolution to the AGM and having it adopted by two-thirds of the delegates, voting on behalf of their individual Institutes. The timing was propitious in that, although the war was still in full swing, the tide had turned in favour of the Allied forces, and many believed that the following year would see landings in France and the beginning of the end of the conflict. People were looking beyond the grim present to a much brighter future, and were determined that their lives would be different and better. As the 1945 general election was to show, change and renewal were in the air.

WIs nationwide discussed the idea of their own college with mixed feelings. Lady Denman herself, still NFWI Chairman, had now become a little dubious. 'Do you really think the members want a college?' she asked. 'Will they come?' But the enthusiasm of those within the National Executive who were pro-college was overwhelming and, although the flying bombs in 1944 made London too dangerous for an AGM to be held, the resolution, put forward by the Oxfordshire Federation, beat off scores of rivals to be one of fourteen resolutions on the agenda in 1945.

Lady Denman had refused to give the National Executive's blessing to the resolution, preferring to leave it to the Institutes to make their own decision without being prodded from the centre. Lady Brunner's proposal of the resolution on behalf of the Oxfordshire Federation was focused, enthusiastic and full of her vision for a college that would attract younger members and open new vistas to older ones, that would offer

'… just for once in a lifetime, mother goes off for two days or even, giddy thought, for a week to mix with WI members whom she has never seen, and listen and discuss and talk her head off with them about bottling or schooling or housing or hospitals from morning to night …'

courses on practical skills but also on cultural subjects that would be new to many who chose to explore them, that would teach and instruct but also be friendly and fun. As she herself admitted in her speech, 'I am afraid that quite a number of us here today may have been put off by the phrase "adult education", and even by the somewhat formal and severe word "college" … There is something a bit intimidating about the former – and grim about the latter.' There was indeed opposition from a number of Federations who felt that it would benefit only a few of their members and that it would be better to increase collaboration with existing educational institutions. The Shropshire delegate felt that it was not fair 'to ask the ordinary member to raise money for something from which she will on the whole receive no direct benefit. It will be for the few, whereas the money will be raised by the many.' And from East Kent: 'Only 3,000 would be able to come in a year, and 300,000 women are being asked to contribute.'

However, the majority of delegates were in favour. The Gloucestershire contingent argued that 'We want to do more than welcome the suggestion; we want to get started. We do not want this college when we are all so old we have to be taken in bath chairs to it; we want it now.' South Stoke WI, Oxfordshire, proposed an amendment to the resolution that 'instructs the Executive Committee to make the necessary arrangements'. As they said 'Who knows, the right house in the right place may be discovered at any moment … How grievous it would be if the executive were not in a position to be able to clinch a deal … We must work quickly if we are to bring our plans of a brave new world into being … Please get going with it at once.' The amendment was carried, and the AGM voted overwhelmingly for the new college.

Financial matters had only been glanced at. Those charged with implementing the resolution now had both to find the right house and to raise the money to buy it, furnish it, maintain it and set it up as an educational enterprise. The Institutes were approached for fundraising and also practical help; the Isle of Ely, for instance, made an early offer to be solely responsible for furnishing a room, an idea that was taken up enthusiastically and remains the practice today. But finding a house was proving difficult, even though the end of the war meant that many large country houses requisitioned for government use were coming on to the market. At the 1946 AGM, it could not be reported that suitable premises had been found, although fundraising efforts had been successful. But the bombshell to hit this AGM was that Lady Denman had decided to step down after nearly thirty years as Chairman. Her soon-to-be successor, Diana, Lady Albemarle, paying tribute to the illustrious record of her predecessor, announced that the most popular of the suggestions as to

Right Students on a needlework course.

Elizabeth Brunner
(1904–2003)

Above Lady Brunner
at the 1952 AGM.

Born into a famous theatrical family, Elizabeth Irving – granddaughter of Sir Henry Irving – seemed destined for an acting career, and indeed was playing Titania in the West End by the time she was sixteen. But a throat problem led to her giving up the stage, and marriage to Sir Felix Brunner and the arrival of five sons directed her priorities elsewhere. Her ascent up the WI ladder was swift: after joining in Henley, she was very soon elected to the Executive Committee of the Oxfordshire Federation, then co-opted on to the National Federation's Education Subcommittee, and after only a year was elected to the National Executive. Lady Denman had been the talent-spotter, seeing in Elizabeth Brunner the idealism, vision and drive that the WI would need in the post-war years.

Lady Brunner went on to be NFWI Chairman from 1951 to 1956, and continued her involvement in Denman for the rest of her life. Many of the furnishings in the main house were gifts from her and her family, and her portrait by R G Eves hangs in the Drawing Room, on permanent loan. She celebrated her ninetieth birthday at Denman in May 1994 with a special lunch party, and paid tribute to what it had become: 'What a joy it has been to see my friends glow when they recall the College of the 1940s and realise with proper pride the high standard to which it has been brought. If anyone had any doubts, they had only to see the warmth and enthusiasm of the students themselves to be reassured for the future.'

Her son, Sir Hugo Brunner, who was Lord Lieutenant of Oxfordshire between 1996 and 2008, continues to take a strong interest in Denman, and has been generous in his support. He has taken part in study days when he has talked about his mother alongside Anne Stamper, Denman archivist, who discussed Lady Brunner's life in the WI. The study days finished with a trip to Grey's Court, the family home, now in the care of the National Trust.

Left An embroidery class taken outside, 1950s.

Above Doris Cummings teaching a cooking class, 1953.

how Lady Denman's name could be forever remembered within the WI was that the new college should be named after her. Lady Denman was delighted, and Denman College was christened.

Shortly afterwards, a Berkshire member telephoned to say that her estate agent husband had on his books a property that she thought might be suitable: Marcham Park near Abingdon, then in Berkshire and now in Oxfordshire. Lady Brunner and Lady Albemarle quickly visited and found it ideal, though it still bore the marks of Air Ministry occupation during the war. These were minor problems; in all other ways it was highly suitable: in the centre of the country, with good transport links, with room to expand, and near a university. Premises had been found.

The asking price, £15,000, was a figure that the National Executive felt it could afford, and so when the Air Ministry agreed to leave by June 1947, negotiations began. The final price of £16,000 included the house itself, 100 acres of land, two cottages let to tenants, and the kitchen gardens and greenhouses that were let to a local market gardener. An appeal was launched to raise £60,000 to buy, equip and endow the college, £20,000 of which was provided by the UK Carnegie Trust and most of the rest by individual Institutes, which were each asked to raise £9 over three years. By the time the appeal closed in 1953, £66,000 had been raised. In March 1947, the deal was concluded.

A new committee – the Denman College House Committee – was set up to oversee the work needed to turn Marcham Park into the new educational institution, with Lady Brunner continuing as chair. They faced huge problems: the garden was a wilderness, the local builders had no labour immediately available, licences and permits were required for the conversion work they were about to undertake, the war was only just over, and all sorts of regulations and shortages would have to be dealt with. Moreover, although there were very many welcome offers of gifts and help in kind from the WIs themselves, acceptance or refusal would need careful handling. As Lady Brunner remarked, 'That very awkward thing – taste – can be divisive.' A rule was made – still in force – that all offers must be considered by the committee.

A letter found in the stable block, unfortunately neither signed nor dated but clearly written by a builder or surveyor who had been asked to report on the work that would be necessary, must have been written very soon after the purchase of Marcham Park in 1947. The writer appeared to believe that Denman might be planned as the first of several such colleges: 'It is hoped ultimately to have a number of country colleges providing short residential courses for Women's Institute members…'

The letter describes Marcham Park as 'a large stone Georgian house of plain character, standing in its own park … All the work considered

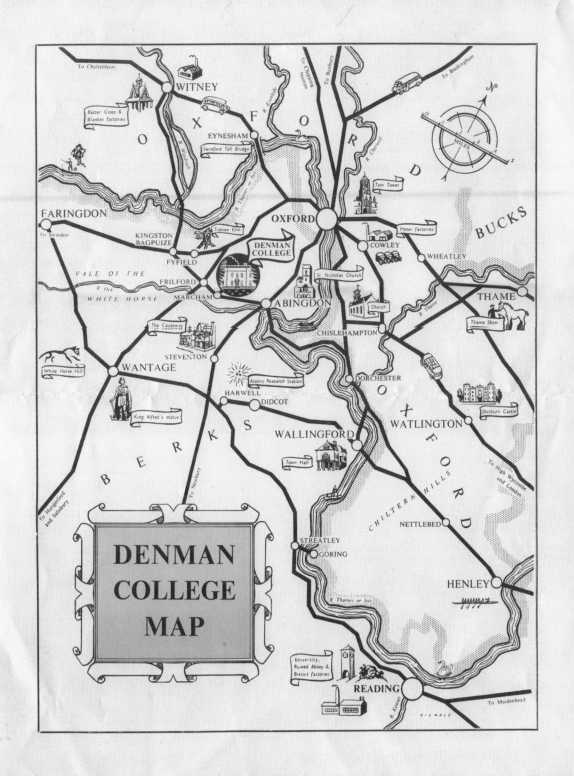

DENMAN
COLLEGE
MAP

Art on display at Denman

As an accredited training college, Denman was entitled to choose works of art from the Victoria and Albert Museum, on loan for up to six months, to adorn its main rooms. Members of the committee took full advantage of this privilege, feeling themselves buoyed up by the recognition that this gave the College. Charlotte Bawden, a member of the Denman committee and wife of the artist Edward Bawden, arranged for the display of pictures by her husband and other contemporary artists at the College.

Not just pictures, but superb pieces of needlework and rich rugs were loaned by the V&A. A jug (right) designed by Eric Ravilious – a close collaborator of Edward Bawden – and made specially for the College by Wedgwood can still be seen in the corner cupboard halfway up the stairs in the main house.

Charlotte Bawden's own speciality was pottery. She played an important part in putting on the early arts and crafts courses and was herself one of the first tutors. The Bawden Studio in the Teaching Centre, designed for the teaching of 'heavy craft', especially pottery, is named after her.

Marcham Park

John Elwes was noted for his miserliness and general eccentricity – he is said to have instructed guests as to the best corner of their bedrooms to sleep in to avoid getting wet when it rained.

The estate had its origins in the medieval period as part of the holdings of Abingdon Abbey, but was sold after the dissolution of the monasteries in the sixteenth century to one William Box, a London grocer. It passed through various owners until it landed in the hands of Robert Meggot, a rich brewer. His son John adopted his mother's maiden name of Elwes when he in due course inherited; the earliest record of the house is a drawing in the Bodleian Library, Oxford, where it is described as 'the seat of John Elwes who died in 1789'. Elwes was noted for his miserliness and general eccentricity – he is said to have instructed guests as to the best corner of their bedrooms to sleep in to avoid getting wet when it rained – but his granddaughter Emily brought a touch of romance to the family when she eloped to Gretna Green with the local MP, Thomas Duffield. 'Our enterprise,' Thomas noted, 'was most hazardous but executed by all parties in a most superior style.'

It was Emily and Thomas Duffield who built the present house in the early part of the nineteenth century, and it was probably also they who planted many of the magnificent trees in the grounds. Sir Thomas Lawrence's portrait of Emily hung in the College until 1963, when it was returned to the Duffield family.

The Duffields owned the estate until 1938 when it was bought and modernised by Geoffrey Berners, who installed the fine eighteenth-century staircase, which came from a house in London, and the chandelier in the Drawing Room. He also built the stable block, which was destined never to be used for horses, and later, as Old Croft, extended the accommodation available at the College. However, he never lived at Marcham Park, which in 1939 was requisitioned by the Air Ministry. Now the Duffields have a renewed stake in the estate, having bought back some of the land when the College wished to sell in the 1970s.

to be immediately essential is covered by the present estimates. The amount of necessary alteration to the house itself is surprisingly small. Apart from a certain amount of remodelling to provide a suitable dining hall and service arrangements, it is limited to the increase (by subdivision) of bedroom accommodation, with a few additional bathrooms, etc. There are at present about fifteen bedrooms and they can be subdivided quite easily to provide a total of twenty-eight small rooms. What is very unusual in such cases is that this increase can be procured without cutting any new windows, except on the attic floor where three new dormers are required. And the original provision of bathrooms is so generous that, while doubling the number of beds, we have only to increase the number of baths and WCs by two baths and three WCs. The main ground floor rooms will serve as lecture rooms without alteration. The greatly increased number of bedrooms necessitates, of course, adjustments with regard to radiators, domestic hot water, and sewage disposal, and a small amount of electric lighting alteration, also increased water storage.'

The writer goes on to detail the work required to turn the stable block into accommodation, and then addresses the provision of practical teaching facilities. 'For the more practical demonstration work – cooking, handicrafts, etc – it is hoped eventually to build a "demonstration Women's Institute" near the house. But as this cannot at present be attempted, it is proposed to make use of a large block of huts used as offices by the Air Ministry. These huts are poor in standard, but they represent about 4,500 square feet of covered floor space, and although the necessary expenditure may be high in relation to their actual quality, it would obviously be quite impossible to provide a similar amount of accommodation in any other form for anything like this price. Fuller particulars of the work required under each of these heads are appended …'

Applications for building licences were turned down, one after the other, so the committee decided to make the best of the house as it was. By cramming beds into as many rooms as possible, they felt that thirty students could be accommodated. Many of the County Federations that had offered to take on the furnishing of individual rooms now fulfilled their promises – though at this early stage, the larger rooms had to be shared between counties. Gifts and donations poured in, and not just from WIs, to the extent that the committee found that they had money left over in the budget allocated to furnishings. This surplus money was quickly allocated to the garden and grounds, which were proving more problematic and expensive than had been expected, though the new gardener, Mary Clarke, was able to start work by April 1948 with two German prisoners-of-war to help. By the summer, the house was

Left The newly opened College ready for visitors, c.1949.

Opposite left The College's first staff, with Betty Christmas seated left, c.1949.

Opposite right A student sketching Christmas Cottage, 1980s.

Applications for building licences were turned down, one after the other, so the committee decided to make the best of the house as it was.

considered fit to be seen, and a full-scale private view – called Operation Frolic – was laid on for 750 AGM delegates. Other open days followed, so that by the end of the year some 10,000 WI members had been able to visit their new college.

The official opening was fixed for 24 September 1948. Thoughts now turned to the appointment of the first Warden – a title used by the heads of a number of Oxford colleges – and it was decided that Elizabeth 'Betty' Christmas would be the ideal person. Although not academically qualified, she had proved herself full of intelligence, organising ability, enthusiasm and friendliness, and she had been very successful as NFWI General Organiser for eight years. Her first staff consisted of just two women in the office – Christina Beckton as College secretary and Barbara Lilley as Warden's secretary; and four on the domestic side – Agnes Messer as housekeeper, Bertha Parker as cook, and two Swedish girls who had come to learn English and decided to stay on to help set up the new college. There were also the gardener, Mary Clarke, and her helpers. Apart from Barbara Lilley, they all lived on site; the Warden eventually, after it was made fit for purpose, in the cottage that still bears her name.

The date of the opening ceremony had been arranged to fall on the day after the WI's AGM in London, so that delegates from all over the country could travel on to be part of the inauguration. Fleets of buses brought some 250 people, welcomed by Lady Albemarle, NFWI Chairman, and addressed by Sir Richard Livingstone – who is pictured and on record as having cut the ribbon across the front door as close as possible to one of its ends because his Scots blood rebelled at the thought that such a magnificent ribbon could not be used again.

As he said in his speech 'Education is not schools or schooling. Its purpose is to assist us to do the things we want to do, and cannot do without help … You may think that one can't do much in a week or a weekend … but one can make the most difficult step in all study – a beginning – and carry on studying at home. One can widen one's horizons and let light into one's mind.' When Sir Richard visited the College again on its fifth birthday, he described it as 'a magnificent thing done in a magnificent way'.

Denman has always been about the importance of providing lifelong learning opportunities for the personal development of countrywomen in their own environment; and while both WI and the College have opened their arms to a wider audience and have in recent years encouraged urban participation too, Denman remains a resource for everyone who seeks to benefit from what it can offer. In the same way that, from the beginning, the Women's Institutes were open to

Above Crowds gathering outside the main house following its opening, 1948.

Right Planting a tree to mark the College's fifth anniversary, with Home Acres in the background. (l–r) Sir Richard Livingstone, Betty Christmas, Lady Brunner and Betty's dog, Sam.

The pre-Denman Denman course

**Peggy Palner, Hempton WI, writing in
the Norfolk WI *Gazette*, December 1992**

In May 1946, twenty-four years old in my last year of teacher training and preparing to be married in July, I was allocated a place on the NFWI Summer School to be held at Somerville College, Oxford, in early July. My kind fiancé, having seen what was on offer, insisted that we should see the rector immediately and move the date of the wedding, so that I might avail myself of this opportunity of a lifetime. Consider the cast list for this week, which was called Leisure and Pleasure. To lead us through the visual arts were Hugh Casson and Lady Rothenstein, wife of Sir John Rothenstein, then Director of the Tate Gallery; literature and drama were to be covered by Dame Rebecca West, along with a visit to the Shakespeare Memorial Theatre, Stratford. To introduce us to good design in everyday living was the director of the newly set up Design Centre in the Haymarket. But the Music Day! Thomas Armstrong, Professor of Music at the University of Oxford, and Ralph Vaughan Williams, whose music had given me so much delight since my schooldays.

So off I went. I shared the taxi from Oxford station with a lady from Northumbria, the wife of a shepherd who had never left her county before and had brought her bagpipes with her; the other passenger was a doctor's wife from Devon. We were met at Somerville by the usual sounds of a gathering of WI members from far and near, a cup of tea, and a quiet welcome from Elizabeth Christmas who was to be the Warden of the proposed WI college when a suitable home had been found for it. Lady Brunner, who was leading the course, welcomed us after dinner. We were divided into working parties who met after each teaching session to discuss what we'd heard and the ways in which we could use our newly gained knowledge to widen the experience of WI members in our counties. The weather was glorious. The company was exhilarating. The lecture sessions were heady stuff for one so young, and yet it seemed perfectly natural to be in the same discussion group as the shepherd's wife and Lady Albemarle, NFWI Chairman. It seemed natural to tell them that wedding plans had had to be altered, and very soon the entire course knew, and I was taken into corners over coffee and given all kinds of advice. Even Dame Rebecca joined in and took me to the library for a little 'quiet session'. She had, I remember, a disconcerting habit of talking with her eyes tightly shut and suddenly flicking them open when one least expected it.

It was all memorable, but the Music Day was the one that remains vivid. In the morning, Dr Armstrong spoke to us on the development of musical forms and, in the evening, we sat in a sun-filled Senate House and listened to his own group of madrigal singers. It was magical. During the teaching session we heard Vaughan Williams talking about writing for amateur music-makers. The choir at my Institute was wrestling with a cantata for women's voices composed especially for WIs, and when it was question time I told him that we were having trouble with a certain musical phrase. 'I'll see you over coffee after lunch and go through it with you,' he said. I can remember walking up and down the lawn with a large, hairy paw on my shoulder while he 'tum-tee-tummed' how the phrase should go. I am sure that other people must have seen a glowing light round me. I was absolutely enchanted, and I can't remember a word he said.

One afternoon late in the week, Lady Brunner and Lady Albemarle went out and brought Lady Denman back to tea. They had been house hunting and they had FOUND THE HOUSE, and now all those years later I was there again. Again, a welcome of tea and the calm, serene face of Elizabeth Christmas, albeit a portrait now. The same happy babble of people getting to know one another. Lady Brunner was there too in the Drawing Room, and as I sat alone there one sunny afternoon, I felt that I must share this experience with others on my course. So, on the last evening, when we'd put work behind us but were still immensely stimulated by clever girls making us excited about mundane things like packaging potatoes, lids and labels and cakes, I told my story.

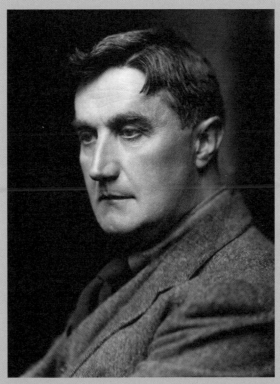

Above Hugh Casson, 1950.

Top right Ralph Vaughan Williams, c.1920.

Bottom right Lady Rothenstein, 1938.

all classes, creeds and persuasions and were democratically run, so Denman is for every WI member. As the host often says during her introductory talk to new course members, the words 'not for the likes of us' have no place here. It is 'our place', special and friendly, offering everything of the highest quality – tutors, accommodation, food and surroundings. Moreover, before the College existed there was no way in which WI members from around the country could get to meet their fellow members, often even those from the same county. Now County Federation weekends offer the chance to mingle with close WI neighbours; and the start of every course involves students who have often come on their own introducing themselves and chatting to fellow WI members whom they have never met before and probably won't see again. As so many of them say, 'I can come here on my own, and feel welcome and safe.' Denman started with that approach and those ideals and it continues with them to this day.

Opposite left Students unwinding and laughing in the Common Room in the evening, 1950s.

Opposite right Students on their coffee break, 2000s.

Above Betty Christmas serving tea during a break in one of the few early courses where husbands were welcomed, *c.*1955.

College Chairmen and hosts

College Chairmen – now called hosts – have been a Denman institution from the beginning. There is and always has been a volunteer host on duty to meet course participants as they arrive, to ensure that they all know how Denman works, to take them on a tour of the buildings, to deal with problems and complaints, and generally to make their stay at Denman as happy and fulfilled as possible. The hosts have their own bedroom and bathroom on the first floor of the main house, with a splendid view over the park; the refurbishing of the room was a parting gift to Denman from Helen Carey, NFWI Chairman from 1999 to 2003. Above the fireplace is a quilt made by Pat Lumsdale, Craft Adviser, just one of the many artefacts in the house made and donated to Denman by supporters over the years.

There used to be two hosts on duty from before breakfast until the last guest left the main house at night and the front door could be locked, but now that there is a night porter there is only one host, who is able to retire early if exhaustion sets in – as it often does. Indeed, at times of crisis, such as occurred in 1959 when the College lacked a Warden and a number of both senior and domestic staff, the Chairmen were pivotal in keeping it all going. Lady Dyer, NFWI Chairman at the time, personally briefed the volunteers and made it plain that the job was no sinecure. As one of them said, 'We were told that this was not a rest cure, and neither were we to swan around the College being in authority and contributing nothing.'

Their responsibilities could and can be daunting: there are behind-the-scenes crises to deal with, doctors to be called if a student or tutor is taken ill (there was even once a death on the premises), and hosts have frequently been known to spend the night at A&E. June Ward recalls many mercy dashes to Tesco in Abingdon, once when a woman who had obviously packed hurriedly had come without underwear, and another – rather more seriously – when a student on a patchwork course was clearly very poorly and needed a new prescription which her GP, consulted by phone, faxed down to the pharmacy there. June arrived just as the pharmacy closed for lunch; when it reopened, it immediately closed again for a fire alarm which caused the whole store to be evacuated. She eventually got the pills, and the woman soldiered on to complete the course and sent June a bouquet afterwards to thank her.

Sometimes, the emergencies are domestic. Diana Trotter offered to help one day when the cook had gone home sick, and was left, single-handed, to produce the main pudding for dinner that evening. As she wrote, 'The boss did say thank you as they loaded the really quite smart gateaux on to the trolley, but I got the impression that he'd expected no less from the WI.'

The hosts have always kept a series of notebooks, designed both to flag up issues and offer thoughts about potential problems and how to deal with them, and also to record comments on how their stints on duty have gone. Perhaps inevitably, this being Denman, the comments are mostly full of praise and contentment. See overleaf for a small selection of the entries.

Opposite Welcoming a new student: a set of pictures shot for a 1960s Denman College souvenir booklet.

June Ward recalls many mercy dashes to Tesco in Abingdon, once when a woman who had obviously packed hurriedly had come without underwear …

Entries from the hosts' notebooks

April 1995

Quite the noisiest week I have ever experienced at Denman, with a very happy crowd on the Surrey week. Absolutely no problems – not one complaint. Quotes: 'Every time I come to Denman I think it can't be as good as it used to be – but it is better every time.' 'This is the first time in thirty-four years of marriage that I haven't given home a thought for four whole days.' 'This was the best holiday I have ever had.' And the Chairman enjoyed it too.

Sally Dampney

March 1997

Once again, Denman worked its magic on two members who obviously needed a break from home problems. Great to see them enjoying and being enthralled by their courses and soaking up the friendly atmosphere. Busy courses with everyone getting on well together, wonderful food, and helpful staff.

Anne Selman, Bedfordshire

November 1999

Quite an eventful few days, a tutor was ill and required paramedics, ambulance and hospital. Entertainment in hall worked well and not so stuffy (heatwise, I mean).

Joyce Yeates, Hampshire

July 2001

Torrential rain, lightning and thunder – floods – typical Wimbledon weather. However, our Dorset Federation weekend has been tremendous fun – lots of first-timers all ready to book another course. Magic Denman.

Diana Perry, Dorset

September 2004

Full college, seven courses, two of which were small group bookings and at least a third were first-timers/non-members. Lovely atmosphere, lots of fun – no major problems. Kept very busy as usual. Radio in this room only one channel, so have left money to buy a new one – can't cope without 5 Live.

Sally Ball, Bedfordshire

July 2006

College Chairman, and her husband this time, were happily accommodated in the Northumberland Room where everything was fine except for the non-functioning telephone. No problems – happy students and sunshine every day – nice ending for me as I hand over to Sue, my co-Chairman and GFWI's new Denman rep … Next time I return, in my thirtieth year of Denman visits, courses, chairing, I hope to become a student once more.

Rosemary Bishton, Gloucestershire

April 2007

Great time with no emergencies in the night. Good crowd of students who have all enjoyed themselves. Good entertainment on Sat. Had flood in the teaching area toilets Sat evening, mopped up etc. (I know my place!!) Can't wait to come again.

March 2008

Probably the best time ever spent as College Chairman! – wonderful set of students who enjoyed everything and made the most of everything to the full! We even managed to sort out the shop till after a power cut. I have enjoyed the chance, as Federation Chairman to do this job – rather sorry but this will probably be my last chance to sleep in this room.

Mary Cooper

December 2008

My last time as a Board of Trustee College Chairman – feeling very nostalgic! So wonderful to be with Barbara again, we had such a happy time with each other and the students. Denman is particularly wonderful at Christmas time … and I feel too emotional to write any more!!

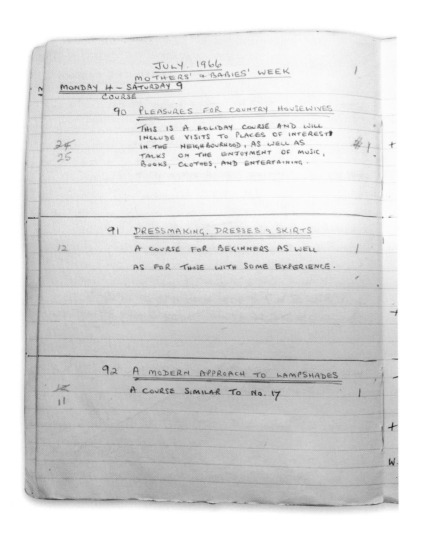

JULY. 1966
MOTHERS' & BABIES' WEEK
MONDAY 4 – SATURDAY 9
COURSE

90 PLEASURES FOR COUNTRY HOUSEWIVES
THIS IS A HOLIDAY COURSE AND WILL INCLUDE VISITS TO PLACES OF INTEREST IN THE NEIGHBOURHOOD, AS WELL AS TALKS ON THE ENJOYMENT OF MUSIC, BOOKS, CLOTHES, AND ENTERTAINING.

91 DRESSMAKING. DRESSES & SKIRTS
A COURSE FOR BEGINNERS AS WELL AS FOR THOSE WITH SOME EXPERIENCE.

92 A MODERN APPROACH TO LAMPSHADES
A COURSE SIMILAR TO No. 17

September 2016

I am sad to say that this is my last visit to Denman as a College host. I came this time with my Federation & travelled by coach otherwise I am afraid my days of travelling by rail are over. That is really why I've had to resign my Denman Ambassador Role.

I really had a wonderful, to me a very loving welcome from Jane Dixon, Denman Head, at the welcome on the first evening. She thanked me for my years of service, do you know, it's sixteen years since I first started. And what years of sheer joy they have been. They presented me with a lovely gift and read out letters from contacts I have made here. One from a very dear friend, Joanne Goxford who has written her account on the previous page. It was very moving & I really felt quite weepy!! Oh dear, I am going to miss all this so much.

Do carry on coming to Denman, friends, support it for all you're worth. We must never ever lose this valuable jewel in the WI crown.

It is my humble privilege to have come here to work as a Denman Ambassador.

This morning as if there were really anything to give me a good send off, one student fell out of bed and damaged her ankle badly. It's a hospital case, but the night watchman, Stuart, very kindly offered to go with her as I was getting rather worried if I missed my coach after lunch, how would I get home?! But again, Denman to the rescue!

Go out always with a bang! Hope she will be fine anyway.
Goodbye Denman, love you forever! X

Jean Lane, Denman Ambassador, College host, Gwynedd/Caernarfon Federation

Denman Representatives and Ambassadors

One of the strengths of the Women's Institutes has always been their independence and their democratic approach to governance. Each Institute is an independent body, yet is also a member of both County Federation and National Federation and subject to clear rules that set out the structure within which it operates. But each also manages its own affairs within that structure, and there are many different approaches to how they work. Members vary too, particularly now that the organisation operates both rurally and in towns and cities. Opinions about Denman can do nothing other than reflect that diversity and that fierce independence.

The College to some extent divided the Institutes from the start, as was evident at the 1945 AGM when many of the delegates spoke for their members with misgivings about its potential reach. 'Not for everyone', 'too far away'; those were some of the opinions then, and those sentiments still find a voice today. Hence the need, from the start, for women who believed in Denman to convey their enthusiasm to their fellow members. These women became Denman Representatives to the Federations, giving talks to the Institutes, organising Federation visits to the College, speaking about their own experience of Denman, often putting members in touch with each other so that they could share transport, and generally promoting the College to the grassroots. They are now called Ambassadors; in some counties, the outgoing Chairman becomes the Ambassador; in others, they are volunteers. Annual seminars offer training in the role and seek to expand its reach.

From the start, it was recognised that financial constraints would prevent many women from participating in courses at Denman. Elizabeth Christmas's first letter to the Institutes welcomed the establishment of bursaries to help those who would not otherwise be able to come, a scheme that continues to this day. These bursaries, balloted for by WI members, are intended to help with both course and travel costs for members travelling long distances to Denman or for those who would be prevented from applying by financial considerations. Many of those attending have been offered a bursary of some kind, and they are often given to members who seem to be especially deserving; Joyce Cormack, for example, who had just lost her husband, was able to take her twin daughters to the first family camping week in 1959 through a bursary and because she was driven to Denman by a fellow WI member.

But it is still the case that scepticism and concerns about the College need to be countered. The Ambassadors are only part of the answer; it is often members returning to their own Institutes and singing its praises who spread the word. As one member described it, 'Once we are through the gates, we forget the outside world and we find ourselves in a sort of "Denman bubble", and we try to take it home with us and try to get our WI friends to become part of it too.'

'Once we are through the gates, we forget the outside world and we find ourselves in a sort of "Denman bubble" …'

EDUCATION AT DENMAN

The 1944 Education Act was a disappointment in some quarters because it failed to live up to the promise in its preceding White Paper to make provision for 'non-vocational post-school education'. However, it did make it the duty of local authorities to 'secure adequate facilities for … leisure-time education … for any persons over compulsory school age who are able and willing to profit by the facilities provided for that purpose'.

Denman was one of several short-stay residential colleges established at around the time to answer that need and to respond to those social and political initiatives – though it was and is unique in owing its existence to, and continuing to be associated with, a national membership organisation rather than a local education authority or a university. It was and remains a member of the association set up to support these new establishments, now called ARCA (formerly The Adult Residential Colleges Association).

The initial foci of the Denman College Sub-Committee, set up in March 1947 to oversee the establishment of the new college, were the practical ones related to the building and the grounds. Who would be responsible for planning the courses was at that stage uncertain. The NFWI already had a sub-committee dealing with educational matters; it was now decided to ask all the specialist sub-committees to put forward ideas and suggestions for 'courses, conferences and other educational activities' to be held at Denman. These ideas formed the basis of the first draft programme.

In May 1948, the first outline syllabus of courses to run from September, after the opening, to the end of the year was sent to all WIs, and members were encouraged to apply for places. There were two main types: 'A' courses, open to all WI members, and 'B' courses, NFWI training courses for those who would become teachers and demonstrators, willing to pass on what they learned to their own and other Institutes within their county or centrally. The 'A' courses were planned and run by the College; the 'B' courses were planned by NFWI Headquarters staff, with those attending nominated by the County Federations. At that stage the College could only accommodate one course at a time, and the first programme consisted mainly of 'B' courses, of the type that the WI had already laid on for some years. There were in fact only three 'A' courses in the first programme: two called Country Housewives and one Christmas course.

There was also an initial 'C' course, by invitation only, but this disappeared almost immediately; and in 1950 a further 'AB' category was introduced, planned by the NFWI, which tended to be more academic in focus; the first of these was Health and Safety in the Home. These categories persisted until the 1980s and were then dropped.

Right Students waving farewell to their tutors travelling in a caravan, *c.*1950.

Opposite A bee-keeping course in the old walled garden, 1960s.

Education at Denman

Below Students on a dressmaking course in Home Acres, 1950s.

Opposite Preparing Christmas decorations in the Drawing Room, 1950s.

The Country Housewives course was the staple of those first programmes, offering subjects such as cookery, gardening and household management alongside brief introductions to cultural pursuits such as music and drama. The planners had little idea in those early days what would attract 'ordinary' WI members to Denman, and persuade them to leave husbands and children for several days or over a weekend at a time when housewives rarely worked outside the home or left their families to fend for themselves. As Lady Brunner later reflected, the course aimed to make participants: 'better cooks and housekeepers … better able to make home more pleasurable. But the aim was always to widen horizons … so, tempted and emboldened, members would quite often book for a specialised course … And for parents whose children were being educated to a degree far beyond what their parents had been, it was a boost. It was seen and could be believed that learning was a lifelong process and gave a new dimension even to grown-ups.'

The official opening of Denman College in September 1948 was also the day of the first course to be held there – a conference for Federation representatives titled The Education of Countrywomen through the WIs. The remainder of the courses between September and December allowed the College to evaluate what would prove attractive for its first full year in 1949 – and already the Country Housewives course was to become only one of a wide range of pursuits with which students could engage.

A letter dated 1 December 1948 from Elizabeth Christmas to WI secretaries announced the 1949 programme. The cost would be 5s per student for tuition plus 15s a night for full board; there were no 'extras'. The courses would be short, so that 'even busy housewives can plan to come'. And it was noted with pleasure that many Institutes were planning to give bursaries or help with travel or accommodation costs so that the College would be accessible to as many potential students as possible. Miss Christmas ended her letter by hoping that 'members from your Institute will be able to come to their own College and find new interests and enjoy meeting other WI members in these beautiful surroundings'.

The 1949 list included four Country Housewives courses, several others focusing on catering, home management and gardening, and two on Pleasures of the Countryside, designed for those who would like to spend part of their holiday at Denman; they offered talks on birds, flowers and country subjects, as well as expeditions to interesting places in the neighbourhood. There was also one on Books and Music, one on Plays and the Theatre, and another on The Story of London. There were only two craft courses, Soft Toys and Smocking (the following

'… for parents whose children were being educated to a degree far beyond what their parents had been, it was a boost …'

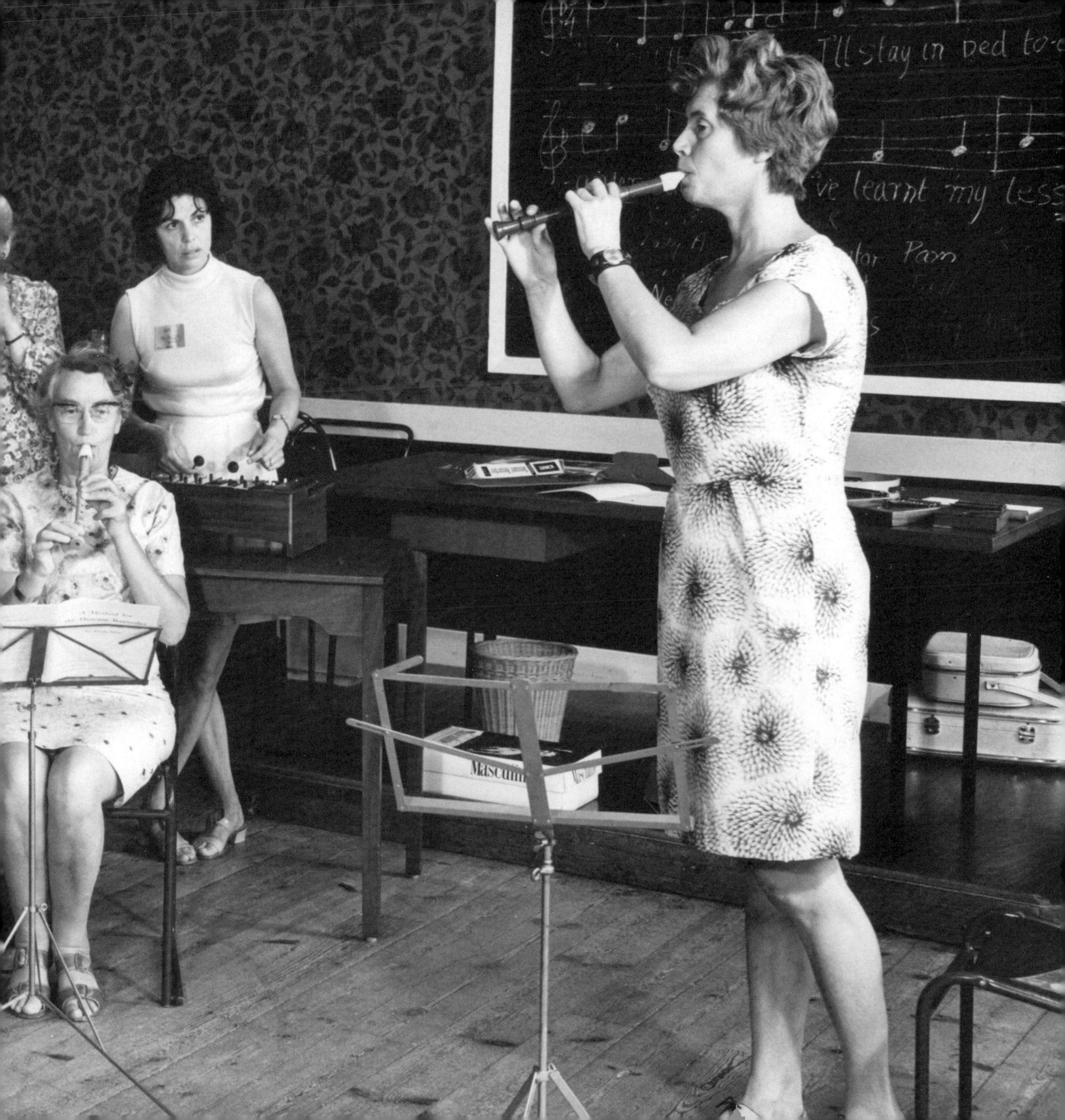
I'll stay in bed
learnt my

year's programme, in comparison, included ten). An annotated copy of the 1949 programme in the Denman archives shows that at least two of the early courses were cancelled, presumably because they did not have enough takers, but that many of the others were attended by more than twenty students. The blurb for Books and Music reassured potential students that they 'should not feel that they must have a wide knowledge before applying, as the purpose of the course is to arouse interest and pleasure'. The planners were clearly keen to dispel the fears of those for whom the words 'education' and 'college' might be threatening. Joan Yeo, a prominent member of the first Denman committee, later said, 'We were trying to see how much academic education the WI would take.'

Within a year or so – especially when more accommodation became available after the conversion of the stables into bedrooms – the College was able to run three courses at a time, but at this stage during weekdays only: two practical courses for twelve students each and one based on lectures for up to thirty. Afternoons were free – many students used the time for reading in the Grace Hadow Library (now the bar) – and there were classes again after tea. There was an optional tour of Oxford on Thursdays, followed by entertainments of various sorts that evening. It soon became clear that more staff were needed to help with the extra workload of both planning and running the courses, so in 1949 a resident Tutor was appointed.

Ten years later, in the prospectus for 1957–58, the cost of accommodation had gone up to £1 a night and the course fees varied, though they were usually 15s, or £1 where individual tuition was offered – and still no 'extras'. The bursary schemes welcomed by Miss Christmas in her introductory letter were flourishing, though the prospectus made it clear that bursaries should be used for 'A' courses only, and that their recipients should not be called on to teach the subject to their fellow

....

My father died in March 2017, and when my sister and I (both Presidents of our respective WIs) went through his old photographs, we came across this one [below]. Written on the back is 'Denman 1950' and it looks as if it was taken just outside the front door of the College. We are pretty certain it came from our grandmother's collection as she was in the WI, as were our two great-aunts. Quite why they were there is a mystery. Their names were Rose Duncan, May Frow and Lena Flower, and we think they are the three ladies kneeling in the front row at the left. They all lived in north Lincolnshire, and one of them must have been President of her WI as we also found a President's brooch. **Rosie Fisher, Duffield Afternoon WI**

....

'We were trying to see how much academic education the WI would take.'

Previous page A recorder class, 1950s.

Left Rosie Fisher's photograph (see above).

Opposite A Russian lesson in the Drawing Room, 1955.

Students in the library
in the 1980s, before the
bar was installed.

54

members afterwards. Always at the heart of education within the WI has been the desire to throw open to all, without strings, the benefits and mind-broadening advantages of learning; there was never to be any compulsion to turn learning into teaching for those who might have baulked at the idea.

This prospectus continued to offer the Country Housewives course, and there were plenty of others centring on cookery, crafts, gardening, home repairs and creative arts such as toy making and puppetry; the puppetry course lasted a whole week and cost 35s with an optional expedition to Stratford to see a play. Other courses included Gothic Architecture (which also lasted a whole week) and Roman Britain, along with Life Begins at Forty, Samuel Pepys and His Times, and Looking Your Best. The programmes did not yet offer courses on what was then considered 'not women's work' such as car mechanics, but it was not long before that sort of skill was also being taught at Denman.

Practical courses remained at the heart of the programme – not least perhaps because 'if a member decided she would come to learn dressmaking or improve her skill in pastry making or preserving, her husband was much more likely to agree to look after himself and the family in her absence than if she proposed taking a course on eighteenth-century literature or modern poetry'. That quote comes from Barbara

I have been to Denman on courses numerous times, usually on a craft course. About sixteen years ago, I decided on a change and arrived on a Friday for a hands-on massage course. There were eighteen of us, and we were in the craft room where the usual furniture had been replaced by nine massage tables. Big signs on all the doors said NO ENTRY. On the Friday evening, the demonstrator asked for a volunteer to have a full body massage. A very brave lady agreed, stripped down to her knickers, and lay on the couch to be massaged. When we paired off the next morning, I ended up with that brave volunteer. It was surreal: lying with just a small towel over your knickers and with others lying on the tables on either side. It reminded me of Silent Witness. I enjoyed being massaged, but found it difficult to start massaging my partner, especially round her boobs. But we all slept well, and at mealtimes people knew straight away which course we were on without asking, from the smell of lavender and our relaxed attitudes. When I went home, I massaged my mother's hands, but I never went any further. **Donna Butcher**

Kaye's book, *Live and Learn: The Story of Denman College 1948–1969* (pp 70–71), published by the NFWI in 1970 to celebrate Denman's twenty-first birthday. It certainly reflects an attitude towards the education of countrywomen that was perhaps over-prevalent in the immediate

The courses on offer at Denman have always been diverse: a car maintenance class, 1950s.

Below Mothers and Babies course, 1950s.

Opposite Family Week at Denman. The 'Lions', a camp team, collecting water and milk, 1960s.

56

Mothers, babies, daughters – and husbands

The Mothers and Babies courses were the brainchild of Cicely McCall when she became Warden in 1957. The first was held in May 1958, offering a choice of courses for the mothers while babies and toddlers were looked after by nurses in the day and by babysitters in the evening. She also introduced in August that same year a Family Week, which included husbands as well as children aged eleven to fifteen, who camped in the grounds under supervision. These courses proved highly popular – so much so that the BBC asked if they could film them – but they put a great deal of extra strain and pressure on the staff. Cots and nursery food had to be provided, extra supervision was needed, and camping in the grounds could be a challenge during a typical British summer. Their undoubted popularity ensured their survival for a few years, but by the early 1960s they had reduced in frequency to just one a year, and were then replaced by a week for Mothers and Daughters (aged fifteen to twenty). Camping was discontinued and the young people were allocated beds in the main house. Mother and Daughter courses were reintroduced in 1994, when a course held over a Mothers' Day weekend saw the College filled with grandmothers, mothers and daughters; there were two parties with three generations and one with four. These courses remain a popular part of the annual programme.

A few early 1950s courses (eg winemaking) were thrown open to the husbands of WI members attending them, and Cicely McCall reintroduced them in 1958, offering weekend courses for husbands and wives. Twenty-six husbands attended that first year, and photographs show them participating in classes such as winemaking and art appreciation. Nora Lewis, who was the housekeeper in the 1960s, categorised the men who came on courses thus: 'There are the good WI husbands, cheerful and good-humoured, ready to lend a hand; then there are the pressed men, wary and not quite at ease, but who usually relax after a bit and admit they are enjoying themselves; and finally, there are the reluctant husbands, deeply suspicious and wondering why they'd ever agreed to be involved.' Sometimes a male tutor is accompanied by his WI wife, and a College Chairman has on occasion booked her husband in for a course while she is carrying out her host duties.

The inclusion of men has not always been without controversy. Some women feel that it is a women's college and that priority should be given to them, particularly if a man takes a place on an oversubscribed course. A husband's presence might also be seen as a constraint on the wife, who may feel anxious for him and therefore less relaxed. And, as some tutors have noticed, men tend to dominate in discussions. However, it has to be said that a man's presence on a course can leaven the company and add an extra dimension. They still come as guests; and whereas it used to be the rule that a man had to be accompanied by a WI member, that is no longer so. There have even occasionally been men who have come alone, having booked themselves on to a course they found compelling.

'There are the good WI husbands, cheerful and good-humoured, ready to lend a hand; then there are the pressed men, wary and not quite at ease, but who usually relax after a bit and admit they are enjoying themselves ...'

My dad passed away in November 2015 and mum came to live with us. It was very hard. Mum kept suffering panic attacks and missed my dad terribly after sixty-six years together. I had read about the Mother and Daughter weekends at Denman and thought that might be something to cheer mum up, so booked us in for the following year. As the weekend approached, mum became panicky again and I wondered if I'd done the right thing, especially as I had booked her into two classes on her own.

What a wonderful weekend we had! Mum has danced all her life (she met my dad dancing in 1949, then aged twenty-nine and feeling that she'd been left 'on the shelf'), and on the Saturday she did the Charleston class. When I dropped a very nervous ninety-five-year-old off in the hall, I explained to the tutor that she was worried about her knees and may like just to watch. But, you've guessed it, as soon as that music started to play she was up and off, learning the routine that the group then performed to the rest of us in the evening. The entertainment was highlighted by the lovely 1920s dresses they all wore. We were also entertained that night by the 'drumming for fun' group, and the wonderful evening was topped off with a live band and ceilidh dancing during which mum happily waltzed round doing the Gay Gordons. By this time, she was quite famous and everyone was commenting on how remarkable she is.

This year I booked us in again. Her panic attacks have gone, but she was still rather nervous about doing two courses on her own as she is partially sighted and profoundly deaf. Did she need to worry? Of course not. At each class were lovely WI ladies who helped her, and the tutors were marvellous at giving her encouragement. No dancing classes this time, but on the Saturday evening 'The Retros' entertained us with music from the 1960s and invited us on to the floor for a twisting competition. 'Come on, mum,' I said, 'we can do the twist,' so up we got, and mum won a prize for 'oldest twister on the dance floor'. Fame again, as a lot of the young daughters said they were too tired to dance and how wonderful to see mum dancing! At our last lunch on the Sunday we happily announced, 'We'll be back.'

Christine Hodges, Worthing WI, Joan Young, mum

post-war years, and was surely responsible for the diffidence of many potential students about coming to Denman. However, there was never a lack of takers for painting and pottery, so things were clearly changing!

Denman had always offered a few courses on what might be termed 'world affairs': Feeding the Hungry World in the 1949 programme attracted twenty-six students, and The United Nations and Ourselves featured in 1958. In the 1966 programme, there was a notably increased range of courses in social studies, history and public affairs, as well as one on Religions of the World and another on World Neighbours. But

the strict non-partisan, non-party-political rule that was enshrined in the WI's constitution tended to restrict the range of discussion possible both within the Institutes and at Denman. By 1971, this approach was being questioned, and a resolution was placed before that year's AGM as to whether the WI should open its meetings to a wider range of topics. Those against change argued that heated discussion of controversial matters might disrupt the friendliness of WI meetings, and that campaigns might be less effective if partisanship or the possibility of succumbing to pressure diluted the message. But those in favour maintained that the WI had always promoted self-education and the broadening of horizons. The resolution was passed, the rule was relaxed, and Denman started to offer more courses on world affairs, contemporary life and controversial issues. There were sessions on topics such as The United Nations, Democracy – its Strengths and Weaknesses, Economics and Ordinary People, Our Common Market Neighbours, The Races of Man, Understanding Political Conflict, and subjects centring on the history of the previous fifty years. Members could also debate Is There a Christian Ethic? and The Morality of Science. And, as Hilda Jones, Director of Studies and then Principal, recalled, 'Those courses were always full.'

In addition to the continuing emphasis on crafts and cookery – the latter now considerably strengthened by the opening of the Home Economics Centre in 1979 – anything to do with Greece, Rome and Homer was popular, along with the Anglo-Saxons. Orienteering and archery were introduced, and there were courses on the Twenties and Thirties, with appropriate parties. Tim Rice came to talk about the planning and composing of *Evita*, enlivening it with insights on choosing the star and the background of putting on a musical. A course on Iran caused a stir when it happened to coincide with the fall of the Shah.

Some students were highly educated and sophisticated, while for others it was a real adventure and they were scared stiff. They often told me that they had hardly dared to come over the threshold but had been so happy to be welcomed by the Warden and the staff. They immediately felt incorporated into the College and their fears vanished. There was one who got lost on her way, arrived at 10pm, and was too scared to press the bell so spent the night in her car. Another one – a regular visitor – drove herself all the way from north Wales in her invalid car. One woman came on a Writing for Children course and went on to be a highly successful, published author, and always said it was because she had had the courage to come on the course.

Hilda Jones, recalling the students she had met during her twenty-year tenure as Principal

Opposite left Mrs K Whitbourn from Sevenoaks, Kent, working on a bowl under the guidance of tutor Donald Potter, 1955.

Opposite right Laying the foundation stone for the Home Economics Centre, July 1978. (l–r) Lady Brunner, Patricia Battishaw, Gabrielle Pike, Lady Albemarle, Hilda Jones and the architect.

Right A souvenir booklet from the 1960s.

Far right A winemaking course, c.1955.

I visited Denman on a weekend course in 1957. At that time, I was a member of Bricket Wood WI, Hertfordshire. I arrived at the house to find my name crossed out on the accommodation list. 'Don't worry,' said the lady in charge. 'We've given you a room in Denman.' It was a lovely room overlooking the garden. I can't remember the name of the course, but it was a friendly group and included a visit to the Astronomy Centre at the University of Oxford where I saw the moon through its large telescope. Another highlight was meeting the Postmaster General from the British base in Antarctica, a speaker on my course. While I was talking to him, he said that if I gave him an addressed envelope he would send me a set of stamps from the base, which he did, and so I have a set of carefully hand-stamped stamps from the Antarctica base in my collection. I remember my time at Denman with pleasure and hope it will continue to be the same for other members.

Joan Hale, Houghton Conquest WI, Bedfordshire

The police, thinking that WI members were likely to be conservative and backward-looking and that therefore the focus of the course was bound to be pro-Shah, warned the College that they might have to face demonstrations by anti-Shah activists. However, as Hilda Jones remarked, 'It was typical that this red-hot subject was covered with sense and composure, and remarkable understanding, dispassion and sensibility.' There were no demonstrations.

In the 1980s, when Denman was rather in the doldrums and its future unclear, fewer students came to the College. The management had changed too, and the programmes reflected a general uncertainty; what was on offer was decidedly 'different'. Country House weekends were introduced, and study tours, two of which were abroad; they did not survive within the schedules for very long at that stage. The course on astrology was never repeated. But many of the old favourites continued, and Denman both survived and got stronger. The success of the Save Denman appeal in 1988 secured its future, and during the 1990s the programmes stabilised and showed a better balance. The nature of the courses had for some time been broadening, with the cookery programme, for example, including many more world cuisine options. So now, while the staples continued to flourish – though Underclothes had become Lingerie – there was more dance, more health and fitness, alternative therapies were on offer, and car mechanics became a regular. There were courses for beginners, intermediate and advanced students; and courses on the use of word processors and the internet would soon become increasingly prominent. Study tours abroad were reintroduced in the 1990s: 1999 saw a painting tour to Greece and a cultural study

The soundtrack to *Evita* by Tim Rice and Andrew Lloyd Webber. Tim Rice came to Denman to give a talk about its composition.

Course planning

The opening of the Teaching Centre and the Home Economics Centre meant that, in the 1970s and 1980s, course planning became much more complex. During those decades, when there was still only one course brochure a year – which did not give the names of the tutors – November and December saw the beginnings of the giant jigsaw that was involved in settling on and fitting in the 200 or so courses planned for the next year but one. When the outline was ready, the Denman College Management Committee, later the Educational Coordinating Group, met to discuss it and to consider new courses. Prospectuses were posted out to the WIs in June, with the deadline for applications in August – a tight timescale that led to the idea that it was no good applying for a course at Denman because it was always full.

In August, a team of some twelve volunteers – who came back year after year – embarked on ten days of frenetic activity, taking up residence in the College and working from 7am till 10pm with occasional breaks for a breath of fresh air and a walk round the lake. Some were conducting ballots for oversubscribed courses, others were writing them into the schedules, yet others were compiling the (usually lengthy) waiting lists. This was early in the development of computers, which in due course radically altered the process – though when computer help was first explored, the experts agreed that computers could take over much of the work, but not the fine-tuning needed to ensure, for example, that friends from different parts of the country could attend the same course.

Today, the publication of three brochures a year allows a great deal more flexibility, for both students and College, and it is frequently the case that late applicants can be accommodated. And of course, the increasing sophistication of the College's computer systems has streamlined the whole process.

Sorting applications while the College was closed for the week, early 1970s. Standing back left are Helen Anderson (Warden) and Hilda Jones (Director of Studies).

'We went to bed with our minds in
a whirl and, not being able to sleep,
decided at 3am to make a cup of tea
and demolish a bar of chocolate!'

tour to Vienna, for example. They continue to this day, and are always full despite the necessarily higher cost.

In some ways, the current 2017–18 prospectus, now that the College can accommodate eighty-three students plus seven tutors and the host, bears a closer resemblance to the one for 1957–58 than to those of the 1970s and 1980s. Simply put, students still want to come to Denman to learn, but television and the internet now provide all one might want in terms of current affairs, politics and engagement with the wider world, and emphasis on leisure and fun is an important part of the mix. The same dynamic operates here as within the WI as a whole: the companionship of like-minded women and the enjoyment arising from making and doing things well are key to why women join the WI and come to Denman; and older and younger women are eager both to preserve and use the ways in which things were done in the past and to learn more about what the old crafts have developed into in the present. The popularity of TV cookery and craft programmes like *The Great British Bake Off* and *The Great Sewing Bee* has led to an increased market for courses in how to do such things. Denman is, after all, one of the few places in the country where women can still learn how to make rag rugs or willow garden creatures.

Cookery and crafts therefore still predominate, offered both as day schools and as residential courses; and much of the tuition would not cause a raised eyebrow among the 1948 or 1958 students: Festive Baking, Let's Make Cheese, Curing and Preserving, Church Flower Arranging, Embroidered Landscapes, Pastels for Beginners. Others are a clear indication of how both Denman and the WI have extended their reach: Baking Jewish Breads, French Bistro, Moorish and Middle Eastern cooking, Trattoria Classics, Calligraphy for Improvers, Tunisian Crochet, Fascinators: an Introduction, Mosaics. And the Lifestyle section continues to offer a whole raft of detailed courses on history, heritage and the appreciation of music, art and literature, along with Cryptic Crosswords for Beginners, Singing: Summer with the Beatles, iPad for Improvers, and a range of genealogical sessions.

Costs have, of course, increased. The all-in prices, for both tuition and accommodation, vary in the 2017–18 prospectus from around £100 for a day school to more than £500 for a course lasting several days. But one can immediately see what huge value for money those prices offer: the costs for residential courses include fine en suite bedrooms, three meals a day with plenty of choice, coffee, tea and cake during both morning and afternoon breaks – not to mention the highly addictive Denman shortbread, which is said to contribute hugely to the 'Denman pound' that staff and frequent visitors inevitably gain in weight. Most of the cost of the courses clearly goes on top-quality

The Great British Bake Off's Paul Hollywood at a cookery demonstration as part of the Real Jam Festival at Denman, 2012.

We spent many happy times at Denman – but March 2008 was particularly memorable. This was our first goldwork course with Hazel Everett, and on the first evening the twelve of us were told about the materials and metallic threads we would be using, and we had to decide which design we might like to do. We went to bed with our minds in a whirl and, not being able to sleep, decided at 3am to make a cup of tea and demolish a bar of chocolate! This enabled us to decide on our design, get a couple of hours sleep, and be ready to begin on Tuesday morning.

This was a week of very high winds and also the Cheltenham Gold Cup. At lunch on Wednesday, we were told that, as the racing at Cheltenham had been cancelled, we might have a visit from a Channel 4 TV crew. We thought they probably wouldn't come, but they did! There was a horse called Denman running in the Gold Cup on Friday, so they thought it appropriate to visit Denman College.

The crew arrived and proceeded to film us. The producer decided that the presenter, Marietta, should be filmed looking as though she was doing some sewing on Elizabeth's goldwork. Laughter erupted as Marietta settled on the chair and adjusted her miniskirt to accommodate the hands-free sit-on embroidery frame, which she likened to riding a horse. More laughter when the male producer had to tell her which way to use the needle! Marietta then went on to interview one of the College Chairmen, Frances, who did a brilliant off-the-cuff promotional plug for Denman College. They also filmed the painting class next door and then they all joined us for a cup of tea. To finish off, we all gathered around Hilda, a ninety-seven-year-old student, to shout 'Good luck, Denman'.

On returning to our room, Elizabeth phoned her husband with instructions to place a £10 bet on the horse called Denman. Her husband was not sure about this but, like all good husbands, did as he was told! With delight, we heard that Denman had won the Gold Cup and felt that Denman College was also a winner that day. The golden thread that linked us with Denman and the Cheltenham Gold Cup also links us all together through Denman and the WI.

June Parrett, Box Hill Evening WI
Elizabeth Fisher, South Godstone WI

tutors and tuition; and still the only 'extras' are some of the materials used in the craft classes and alcohol bought from the College bar. Since 2001, non-members of the WI have been welcome too, for a small additional cost; the year after this was introduced saw 227 non-members coming to Denman.

In the early years, Denman appointed course Chairmen as well as College Chairmen, whose job was to host and coordinate the courses

Sewing and embroidery classes have always been a mainstay at Denman.

Denman workshops

In 1973, the NFWI announced a new initiative: it wanted to hold a workshop at Denman, with the aim of exploring and spreading the word about a major project, pooling ideas and encouraging the Federations to take up the project and make it their own as they chose. The first one was to centre on European Architectural Year 1975 – itself a new initiative involving 'years' devoted to broad themes. Thirty-two Federations sent representatives, and they learnt about the government's plans for conservation areas, how to find out about local plans, grants and funds available for environmental improvements and tourist projects, and how to learn more about their own areas. The workshop resulted in a great deal of enhanced local work; in East Sussex, for example, several WIs produced booklets of village walks, some of which were published by their local county councils. Other successful workshops followed at Denman, testament to the role of the College in promoting new ideas to the Federations and to individual WIs all over the country – the manifestation of the ripple effect that Denman causes as ideas nurtured here spread out widely.

and look after the visiting tutors. In addition, they were expected to link the courses with the wider work of the WI – something on which Lady Denman was always particularly keen. As she wrote in 1949, 'Something of the work of the NFWI should always be included.' Links should be recognised and emphasised between the content of a course and both the everyday experience of WI members and larger issues tackled nationally; for example, a course on an architectural subject could be linked with the WI's work on rural planning and the safeguarding of ancient buildings, and one on books with the AGM resolution on county library services. Above all, she insisted, 'The dual purpose of the movement – the improvement of social conditions in rural areas, and the bringing of knowledge, skill and enjoyment to individual members' should be pointed up as part of the Denman experience.

Denman has always also operated as a WI training centre. The College has run courses for what were once known as WI Voluntary County Organisers (now WI Advisers), as well as for tutors, judges, demonstrators and assessors. The 1957 programme included courses on How the WI Gets Things Done, one of which included a day spent at the London AGM, and others for WI officers and committee members. There is specific training for Federation Chairmen, Secretaries, Treasurers and Trustees, including leadership and financial skills, as well

I have been a member of several WIs as we moved round the country, starting in 1964 when I was told that if I wanted to get to know people in my new home I should join the WI. I liked what I found going on there, and it has been a major part of my life ever since. I have attended several courses at Denman, including a philosophy course when I was joined for dinner and the evening lecture by my daughter, then studying PPE at Oxford.

A one-off course was Teaching Adults, which involved two weeks separated by some teaching practice and resulted in a nationally recognised qualification. This opened up a new part-time career for me, involving leading courses called Walking the Ridgeway and Walking with a Map. A major project was helping to organise walking the North Downs Way, forty miles west to east across Surrey, with the route split into ten sections, five mornings and five afternoons with different distances and difficulty. WIs along the route provided teas and a WI husband with a coach offered transport. Hundreds of members, aged between seventeen and eighty-two, took part. As I have certainly found out, one thing within the WI often leads to another; and 'Join the WI and learn a new skill' could not be more true.

Joy Morgan, member and executive member of several WIs and County Federations

Right iPad courses have enjoyed great popularity in recent years.

Judges testing students'
baking efforts in the
Livingstone Room under
the Country Housewife
Mural, 1950s.

as for independent financial examiners who help WI Treasurers and audit accounts. These courses continue, and today the NFWI Unit in the grounds is the base for the organisation's cookery, craft, training and other committees.

The College is also at the centre of a wide range of countrywide learning opportunities organised by the Education and Training working groups and other committees based in London and Cardiff in conjunction with the Federations. A national travelling tutor scheme enables tutors in a wide range of subject areas to provide classes and day schools in the Federations organised by coordinators based in six areas round the country. These Linked Learning Opportunities are available for WI members in more than 8,000 WIs and seventy County or Island Federations throughout England and Wales. Several of the courses provided at Denman have, in addition, led to accreditation from other bodies such as the City & Guilds Examinations Board or the Laser Learning Network. These courses involve sessions at the College along with home study supported by learning materials and contact with tutors.

While Marcham Park was being transformed into Denman College in 1948, about 10,000 WI members had the chance to visit their new facility. But once courses started, the College was open for visits only during the annual two-week closure. It was Cicely McCall, in the mid-1950s, who opened it up to weekend visits from WIs. Bookings poured in. So in the early 1960s, Marjorie Moller introduced County Federation weekends, when a Federation would take the whole place over both for courses and for interaction with other WI members in the county. This was primarily seen as a useful way of bringing first-time students to the College – encouraging attendance by women who might be diffident and intimidated by the thought of being seen as slow or stupid, however much they wanted to learn or improve a skill. These weekends were discontinued in the 1970s when the College was always fully booked, but resumed in the 1990s and are a large part of the programme today. The usual format is for the Federations to decide what courses and sessions they would like to be on offer and for the College to book tutors and arrange the programmes. The weekends are also an incentive to the more far-flung Federations to save costs by hiring transport and travelling together. The Denman Travel Fund, set up in 1988 in memory of Agnes Salter, NFWI Chairman 1985–88, provides additional help by allocating the interest every second year to the Federations, offering larger shares to those furthest from the College as encouragement to book themselves in.

'… encouraging attendance by women who might be diffident and intimidated by the thought of being seen as slow or stupid …'

Denman has had an undoubted impact on its students: 'There should be a health warning: this can seriously change your life,' said Vicki Fattorini, whose course on nineteenth-century literature at Denman led to her enrolling on an Open University foundation course. Other students have said, 'I left school without taking O Levels … I hadn't realised just what a large part Denman has played in my thinking, in my education and learning, and in my enjoyment of life.' 'Every time I have been, I have been encouraged to explore aspects of whichever craft I was interested in that I didn't know I was capable of.' 'I hadn't done much history; then I attended a course on William the Conqueror and got enthusiastic. I am now working on an access course at the local university, Relating the Past to the Present … and what about the fun and the friendship!'

Denman upholstery, August 2017

Five WI members who took the upholstery class taught by Joanna Heptinstall in August 2017 share their WI and Denman experiences.

Janet Bates, from Ravenshead WI, has been a member for about ten years. She was encouraged to join by her mother, who was a long-standing WI member, and came to Denman for the first time in 2016 for a calligraphy course.

Elaine Gilligan, from Broughton (Preston, Lancs) WI, visited the WI tent at a local show out of curiosity. They were so friendly that she decided to join, but it took a while to find a WI in her neighbourhood where she felt comfortable. She first came to Denman with friends to do a course on silver jewellery, and then to one on dolls, and she came to this upholstery course on her own, being sure that she would be made immediately welcome and would not feel at all nervous.

Carole Orgell-Rosen of Didsbury WI has been a member for about fifteen years, and was initially attracted by the variety and companionship on offer. She has been to Denman several times, taking courses on tai chi, criminal psychology, goldwork and – her favourite – vegetable bakery.

June Ward of South Green (Billericay) WI is the longest standing, having been a member for some thirty years – and it took twenty-five of those years to persuade her sister, Frances Woodruff of Sidmouth WI, to join. Frances says, 'I felt shy and nervous about going on my own, but eventually my husband and daughter escorted me to the door, so that I couldn't back off, and I immediately met two other new members who have been close friends ever since.' The sisters, who live at opposite ends of the country, use Denman as a meeting point, usually coming about twice a year, and have also brought their daughters on courses. June also frequently acts as host.

'They often told me that they had hardly dared to come over the threshold but had been so happy to be welcomed by the Warden and the staff.'

Mrs Farquaharson
dispensing tea during
the tea break, 1950s.

They all agree that WIs differ, and that a new member has to find the right one to suit her. June, in Essex, is aware of several Institutes in her area with different foci, but says also that when a member decided to establish a new one recently, it immediately attracted around eighty women who were either new to the WI or felt that they would benefit from a different approach. All agree too that the younger generation on the whole – there are exceptions, particularly in London and the bigger cities – tend to feel that the WI is not yet for them, though when they come to Denman they enjoy the time spent with their mothers and the other, usually older, course participants. WI members are more than happy to come on their own, and agree that the courses are excellent value for money – though there is also a perception that the WI is about cheapness and thrift, so the cost of the courses can at first sight seem a bit steep. Until, that is, you look at what you get for your money: full-board accommodation in excellent rooms, very good food and, of course, highly skilled tutoring.

Students getting hands-on during an upholstery course, 2000s.

TUTORS AND STAFF

Tutors

The founders' vision was that the College would employ 'the very best lecturers and teachers'. The practical courses would be taught on the whole by NFWI-trained tutors, and it was hoped that the lecture-based courses would attract distinguished practitioners in their fields. They did. 'You really could get anyone you wanted,' wrote Shirley Anglesey, who chaired the Denman committee in the late 1950s. 'The top people in their field were excited by the thought of speaking to countrywomen who hadn't had educational opportunities – people gave their time readily.' Hilda Jones always went to the top when recruiting new tutors, and some of the contacts she made in the 1960s and 1970s were still involved with the College decades later. There were distinguished names: Patrick Moore taught astronomy; the poet Stevie Smith and the artist David Gentleman came to give memorable lectures; and some of the country's leading scientists were happy to share their work and the excitement of science with Denman students.

The modesty of the payment that Denman could offer its lecturers did, however, limit its ability to attract some of the very top names. And the course organisers had to be sure that those invited to lecture were skilled at putting across their often-complex subjects to a lay audience without patronising them or destroying their confidence. Discreet enquiries usually had to be made.

For the practical courses, the College could call upon long-standing WI stalwarts: the Craft Advisers and Home Economics Advisers appointed by NFWI over the years came as tutors, and the first College gardener, Mary Clarke, gave practical instruction and demonstrations in the garden. Many of those trained within the WI system, some of them at Denman itself, came back to tutor. And then there were the remarkable Miss Hutton and Miss Bode who taught cake icing, sweet making and household management. Their connection with the WI went back to the 1943 conference at Radbrook College, where Miss Bode was Principal and Miss Hutton was on the staff. When they both retired in 1948, they immediately became Denman tutors, and continued until 1970 when they were in their nineties. Miss Hutton, who had a wooden leg, would drive them to the College in a very ancient Morris Minor, and though they had to have a survival team to keep them going, the staff felt that they were so extraordinary that they didn't have the heart to tell them that they couldn't come any more.

Educational practice has naturally changed over Denman's seventy-year history, and the short course format offers its own challenges.

Right Patrick Moore, **1966**.

Far right Stevie Smith, **1963**.

Tutors and staff

Original staff members
seated beside the lake
in the College grounds,
1949. Betty Christmas
and her dog Sam are on
the right.

Above A pottery class, 1952. Charlotte Bawden is fourth from the right.

As early as 1955, it was suggested that the lecture – where students just sat and listened – should be replaced with a more interactive arrangement, which does not always come naturally to academics working in a university environment. The tutors have always had to be able to establish an immediate rapport with students they have usually never met before and who are likely to possess a wide spectrum of skills and knowledge – some already with an in-depth understanding of the subject; others, total beginners.

Students have come to Denman because they want to be well taught; tutors have come because they find committed, enthusiastic students who work hard. One tutor in the 1990s was warned by a colleague that he might have to 'make allowances and lower standards' for WI members. Not at all, was his experience: his students approached the subject intelligently, were full of questions and insights, and were committed and diligent.

Denman today attracts tutors of high calibre, who value the excellent, well-equipped teaching rooms and the support of the dedicated staff who set up the rooms, get everything ready, and are on call to help when needed. They also find the short residential courses satisfying to teach, and agree that they can get as much done over two or three days as over a whole term of evening classes because of the continuity. The table set aside for them at meals, and the use of the Nugent Harris Room as a sitting room in which to relax, are also benefits – though the bottles of sherry and whisky that Hilda Jones used to put in the cupboard there for them are a thing of the past!

....

Denman was the kickstart to my career, which began in 1965 when I was appointed Instructress in Charge of Rural Domestic Economy there. I was an enthusiastic but raw recruit straight out of college, so I grabbed this opportunity with both hands and revelled in the welcome, friendship and support given to me by WI members and staff at Denman. This was the perfect springboard for a long and varied forty-five year career teaching food studies. It is difficult to describe how much confidence, enjoyment and experience those early years gave me. And when I was invited to return to Denman after my retirement in 1995 to teach there again, I found the magical atmosphere unchanged, as if it had been quietly waiting for me to come back after all that time. Having now seriously retired, I am still, aged seventy-five, demonstrating cookery to wonderful WI ladies in Dorset. Thank you, Denman.

Susan Bridgen

....

Right A cooking class in the College's state-of-the-art facilities, 2000s. Peter Lien, course tutor, is on the right.

In her magisterial 1997 book celebrating Denman's first fifty years, *Rooms off the Corridor*, Anne Stamper asked the question, 'What kind of a person do you want as the Warden/Principal of the short-stay college that belongs to a women's organisation?' As she herself reflected, the WI had been trying to answer that question ever since Denman opened, and the appointments had varied in effectiveness: 'Some of the Principals have been successful, some have been cherished, some have been both, some have been neither.'

It is clear that Elizabeth Christmas, the first Warden, was both successful and cherished. She laid the foundations of the new educational institution with the help of only two administrative staff: Barbara Lilley, her secretary, and Christina Beckton, the College secretary. In consultation with the Trustees and the overseeing committee, these three women planned, organised and ran the first two years of courses at Denman, until it was recognised that the workload was too heavy and Edith Leathart was appointed as Tutor. But already by 1950, Miss Christmas's health was beginning to deteriorate, and although she carried on as long as she could, she realised in 1954 that she was too ill to continue and resigned.

For a while, the College was jointly run by Barbara Lilley, whose post was retitled Bursar and who was given general responsibility for running the household and estate, and Delphine Dickson, who had become Tutor in 1953. Then, in August 1957, Cicely McCall, who had previously been Education Organiser for NFWI and was involved with Denman at its beginning, became Warden. She was very much a new broom; she felt the College had become inward looking and she wanted to 'let in the light'. She felt it her responsibility to 'get the College going again after its time of retreat from reality during Betty's illness'. She opened it up at weekends to WI visits, she introduced day students, and she initiated a very popular series of courses for whole families. To raise funds and to encourage visits she laid on a huge two-day Flower Festival in July 1958, opened by Constance Spry who also presented the prizes. Marcham was clogged up with the hundreds of coaches driving through the village.

But, as Miss McCall herself later recognised, she had moved too far and too fast. The long-standing staff disliked the new, much busier regime, the NFWI was suspicious of the changes, and the writing appeared on the wall when Delphine Dickson was abruptly replaced by a much younger Oxford graduate. Miss McCall was dumbfounded when

Left Staff and students posing for a photograph, *c.*1950. Betty Christmas is in the centre with her dog Sam, and to her right is Dame Francis Farrer, NFWI General Secretary.

Right Lady Brunner watching on as Betty Christmas cuts the cake for the College's fifth birthday.

Elizabeth 'Betty' Christmas

Denman's first Warden was a long-standing member of the WI, having joined in Bures, Suffolk, when she was sixteen. The daughter of a village postmaster, she was not academically educated but showed a gift for organisation and was soon elected to posts within her own WI and then offered a job at the NFWI. In 1940, she became General Organiser, and in 1945 she was entrusted with undertaking a tour of Canadian WIs on behalf of the Ministry of Information – and the story goes that when the tour was being arranged, the person at the Canadian end was called to the Foreign Office and told off for receiving a cable in code, something that was forbidden. 'Our experts have been unable to decipher it,' the official announced. It read 'Christmas comes in July.'

She was involved with the 1943 conference that resulted in the College being established four years later, and when the question of who should be the first Warden was being discussed, she was seen as ideal. She threw herself into Denman with great enthusiasm, and worked night and day to make it a success. Her health, however, was beginning to cause concern, and the sudden death of her mother in 1950 added to the pressures on her. Her black labrador, Sam – a gift from Lady Brunner – was both a consolation to her and a great favourite with the students.

She was well known for the welcome she gave to the students and her friendliness and approachability. One student later said, 'My main memory of early Denman is of watching Betty Christmas welcoming in women for many of whom this was their first resident visit outside their own village. Betty set a standard for warmth, hospitality and sympathy which is still evident. Her wide smile, shining eyes, and Sam, her large black dog, really made Denman.'

Another comment, however, was that 'she wore herself out because all the members wanted to confide in her and share their problems'. An operation appeared to have been successful, but in 1954 her health again began to deteriorate, and she was forced to spend much of her time either undergoing treatment in hospital or at home in her cottage. Her staff helped her loyally. It was clear that Denman was her life, and there was no question of anyone else taking over while she could do

the work. In the spring of 1955, she learned she was to be awarded the OBE, which she insisted was an honour for Denman not for herself. She organised a party for the staff to celebrate but was too ill to attend it herself. In April 1955, knowing that she wouldn't recover, she resigned and in due course went into a nursing home in Beaconsfield where her connection with the College was maintained by frequent visits from the staff. She died of cancer in November 1956. Her portrait, commissioned by the first four women to work with her at Denman, hangs on the landing in the main house, next to her OBE certificate and medal which were donated to the College by her brother.

Top left Hilda Jones, 1960s.

Bottom left Helen Anderson in the Drawing Room, 1960s.

Above Helen Anderson and Hilda Jones looking through applications, early 1970s.

her resignation was demanded in mid-1958, despite having halved the deficit and doubled the intake of students within a year. Her departure heralded several months of near chaos, with the staff left behind unable to cope and many of them deciding to leave. An advertisement for the post of Warden attracted more than sixty applicants but none was found to be suitable for the job.

The NFWI turned to two people who lived nearby: Lesley Ferguson, a past staff member now retired, and Jan Bateson, a WI member and past Chairman of the Management Committee. They agreed to hold the fort, but only for a few months each. The staffing situation was in such disarray that the closure of the College was seriously discussed. But then Marjorie Moller, a newly retired headmistress who lived nearby, approached the College authorities, was interviewed, and – despite having never been involved with the WI or with adult education – was appointed to the post. 1960 was designated Denman College Year and a new fundraising campaign started which eventually raised more than £40,000.

Miss Moller recognised that the College was at a low point: it was seriously understaffed, and the lack of a single and consistent controlling hand had resulted in enormous strain being put upon those who worked there. She proposed that there should be an additional, full-time, residential post of Studies Secretary. The NFWI agreed, but the first appointee did not stay long, citing 'the strain which working at the College imposed on the staff'. But, in January 1961, Hilda Jones started her long association with Denman first as Studies Secretary, then as Director of Studies, and eventually as Principal.

After the crisis years of the late 1950s, the 1960s were a time of recovery and consolidation. Miss Moller and Miss Jones worked together to establish a successful formula and a mix of courses that resulted in a 60% increase in attendance by 1964, when Miss Moller retired. She was succeeded by Ann Dolphin, who stayed for three years, and then by Helen Anderson. It was during Miss Anderson's tenure that the new Teaching Centre and residential blocks were built, considerably enhancing both the capability of the College to broaden its educational offer and the experience of staying there. She opened up the College to the village too, offering it as a venue for the local WI and the parish council to hold their meetings. As she said in a later interview, 'We thought that the village of Marcham regarded Denman as a bit of a mystery and felt excluded, though some of them worked here, so we held some successful open days, and we were also able to offer accommodation for meetings in the new buildings.'

The ten years of Helen Anderson's wardenship saw the continuation of the fruitful collaboration that had been established with Hilda Jones

The staffing situation was in such disarray that the closure of the College was seriously discussed.

as Director of Studies and, on Miss Anderson's retirement in 1977, Miss Jones was offered the post. However, because she wished to continue with her existing role, she chose to combine the two tasks of educational planning and administration and became the first Principal. Her four years in the job saw Denman continuing to flourish. She described those years in a taped interview during the 1990s: 'My first job was to interview for a new Bursar, and David Austin was appointed. He joined me, along with our secretaries, the course secretary, and a part-time assistant as the total complement of administrative staff. We also had the housekeeper, the cook and an assistant on the domestic side, and a handyman and a gardener, each with a part-time assistant, to manage the buildings and grounds. When I took over, I insisted that I had to have a deputy as well. The first one lasted only six months because, although she was good at the job, she just didn't fit in and at Denman you have to be liked by everyone. I was near retirement, so I struggled on.'

Financial difficulties meant that the College, which at that time was open only every other weekend, had to lay on more weekend courses, which was hard on the staff. The arrangement with Abingdon College (see p116) was proving so inconvenient that thoughts turned to tacking another hexagon on to the Teaching Centre as a Home Economics Centre. Once again fundraising was started, partly enabled by the

celebration in 1978 of Denman's thirtieth anniversary, and the new facility was opened in 1979.

Hilda Jones retired in 1981. 'My final year, 1980, was very significant as we had all-time record numbers. My farewell party was hugely enjoyable, with long-term lecturers and long-term volunteers all coming. My final course was A Background to New York, which was very appropriate as I love jazz and we had New York jazz music to see me off in style.' She and Miss Anderson continued to take an interest in the College; a joint interview with them in the 1990s provides an invaluable insight into the middle years of Denman's history.

The years after Miss Jones' retirement saw another period of crisis. Her immediate successor lasted a mere six months, and even the decision to appoint a Deputy did not seem to result in appointees staying in the role for long; some were clearly the wrong people for the job, and others had to resign for health reasons. The six years between 1981 and 1987 saw seven Principals and Deputies come and go. Staff morale was understandably low. But the arrival of Pauline Brown in 1987, along with Graham Jones as her Deputy, offered hope for a new beginning. She was forthright about her concerns for the College in her report – subtitled 'Reflections on the stench of opprobrium' – to the National Management Committee soon after taking office:

The arrival of Pauline Brown in 1987, along with Graham Jones as her Deputy, offered hope for a new beginning.

Staff in residence

One of the characteristic features of short-stay residential colleges used to be that the Principal and often many of the staff lived on site. This has been true of Denman for much of its history, though it is no longer the case. The last resident Principal was Graham Jones, and before him only one had lived outside the College; she was married with a child, whereas all the others were single. Hilda Jones said that it was the offer of accommodation that induced her to come to work at Denman; and conversely, it was sad for Cicely McCall that she had sold her own house in order to become Warden, only to be rather summarily dismissed after a year.

When the College opened, there were two suites in the main house for the housekeeper and the cook, and Elizabeth Christmas also lived there until she moved into her cottage. The two thatched cottages in the grounds were occupied by the gardeners, and staff accommodation was later enhanced by two semi-detached houses, two bungalows, and a flat for the Bursar in what is now Gwalia.

As the College grew, and the staff complement grew with it, there was much recruitment from the local area and so the need for staff accommodation decreased. By the 1990s, the only residential staff were the Principal, the Deputy Principal (who at one time lived next to each other in the twin thatched cottages), the Bursar and the maintenance man. Now only the maintenance man lives on site. Christmas Cottage is now used for staff when required.

Christmas Cottage.

'Reports always late; figures never produced on time; senior staff never available; gardens overgrown; teaching resources inadequate and non-functional … course tutors double booked; kitchen under pressure … From the manner in which I have been received and the reiterated demand from tutors and course attenders that they hoped I would stay (this without even knowing what I am like), I have begun to realise something of the effect that the turbulence of senior staff has had on the life of this College … I have to ask for a period of stability against which change and development may take place steadily.'

Hilda Jones had deplored the fact that in her time the Denman Management Committee had been disbanded and the educational work was allocated to a sub-committee of the National Federation Education Coordinating Group. She felt strongly that Denman should have its own governing body. This was now recognised, and the Management Committee was reinstated under the chairmanship of Agnes Salter, then NFWI Chairman and a great supporter of Pauline Brown. Continuity was also provided by the Bursar, David Austin, who held the post for seventeen years until his retirement in 1992.

Worries about the future of the College had prompted a Save Denman fundraising initiative in 1988, which raised an extraordinarily generous million pounds and enabled much-needed repairs and refurbishment to go ahead. Staff remained in post and their morale improved. But Denman still seemed jinxed by ill health. Agnes Salter died of cancer in January 1989; cancer also forced Pauline Brown's resignation that year. Luckily though, wanting continuity and to leave the College in safe hands, she made sure that her Deputy, Graham Jones, would succeed her.

The first male Principal – and as it happens, the last to be resident on site – was good for the development of the College, as he had a strong background in adult education and administration. He persuaded the Management Committee to develop a long-term plan for the College, and was able to consolidate the work of his predecessor in rebuilding confidence. Numbers went up as his tenure saw almost continuous opening, offering a wider range of courses. He considerably increased contacts with other local educational organisations and tapped into new sources of funding. By now the College had more than 6,000 students a year, with five courses running at a time, two or sometimes three changeovers of students in a week, and a much larger staff.

Graham Jones' departure in 1997 led to another period of change. His successor, Marilyn Holyoake, came with experience in further and adult education, but never really got to grips with the challenges of a short-stay residential college; she left in 1999.

Opposite Tutor and student in the library on a Thoughts into Words course, 1955.

Right Graham Jones, early 1990s.

Far right Jane Dixon, 2017.

There followed a constitutional review. Denman became a subsidiary charity of NFWI, while retaining its own charitable status and its own constitution and aims. At the same time there was a restructuring of the staff: a new post of Head – later renamed Director – of Education and Training was created to encompass the work of both the College and the NFWI, and Jennifer Adshead was appointed. She had worked at Denman since 1995, first as the Home Economics Tutor and then as Head of the National Training Network. There was therefore now no longer a Principal of Denman whose only concern was the College – though in 2005 the title was modified to include 'Head of Denman' in order to emphasise the importance of that part of the job.

Mrs Adshead oversaw the continued development and consolidation of the College until her retirement in 2007. Her successor, Stephen Hackett, lasted a mere two years. But in 2011, Jane Dixon arrived, offering a varied background in education and a refreshingly business-like and forward-looking philosophy. She quickly saw the need to make radical changes to bolster a somewhat demoralised staff and to question an attitude that was in many ways stuck in the past. She wanted happy staff members offering top-class customer service in a congenial learning environment. She saw the need for more marketing and so set up the first ever dedicated marketing team.

She changed the brand: the cookery courses on offer were to be taught in the WI Cookery School, not in the equivalent of a domestic science college, and New Wave weekends are part of an initiative aimed at reaching out to a younger WI audience. The website and the programmes have been modernised as part of a fully automated business. Both old and new staff now work under her as Head within a flourishing and happy College community.

....

I've been coming to Denman many times in the forty-five years I've been a member of Hawton & District WI. Two years ago, I came on the Nottinghamshire weekend to do flower arranging. When we arrived, our bus driver told us he was meeting the other bus driver when we got there. I walked into the entrance to see a man sitting waiting, so I asked him if he was the other driver. No such luck – he was the tutor for flower arranging. On introduction to us all, he used the comment to break the ice. I came again this year and had him again and he hadn't forgotten. We all enjoyed the class and can't wait to come again if he'll have us.

Jane Timmins, Hawton & District WI

....

Floral Art course with its tutor, David Martin, who is also Courses Manager at Denman.

Funding Denman

Right from the start, the WI knew that financing their College would be a challenge; and there have been several occasions during the seventy years of its existence when it seemed that it could not survive. But there has always been a rescue, and Denman has benefited from a variety of funding sources: direct appeals to the membership; subsidy from the centre; the fees paid by students; bequests and donations; money raised from the sale of land; and a limited amount of governmental support.

The first fundraising campaign was in 1947, to buy Marcham Park and turn it into the new residential educational institution. The Carnegie Trust provided £20,000 and an appeal to the members eventually raised £60,000. The dining room was extended in 1957 after funds were raised in memory of Lady Denman. Members also rallied round when plans were put in place to build the new Teaching Centre and residential block named for the Brunners in the late 1960s, and yet again for the Home Economics Centre ten years later, when they gave Denman £28,000 as a birthday present. The 'Buy a Brick for £5' campaign in the 1990s helped to build five new residences in the grounds.

In addition, generous donations over the years have funded projects like the building of New Croft and a start being made on the new Teaching Centre – which was also supported by Sir Felix and Lady Brunner when it became clear that there would be a shortfall. The sale of land, first the market garden and then a large part of the grounds, not only allowed repair and maintenance work to be undertaken but also enabled the College to establish an endowment fund for the future.

The crises that have hit the College at various times have led to appeals to the membership to secure its future. The 1960 appeal, needed after the uncertainty of the late 1950s, raised more than £39,000, which allowed the College to enjoy a period of stability and consolidation. But it was the extensive building work required in the mid-1980s (see p117) that led to the biggest appeal, when the National Executive Committee unanimously decided that in order to save Denman, £1 million was needed both to carry out the work and to enhance the endowment fund to allow for regular repairs, renewal and maintenance. The whole amount was raised in time for the celebrations of Denman's fortieth anniversary, and finally put the College on a sounder financial basis.

Fundraising, however, will have to continue, because the College cannot be funded out of the regular subscriptions, which are always over-committed to both the NFWI's and the Federations' other educational work, as well as to all the other activities that the organisation undertakes. There are regular 'Do It for Denman' events: in 2006, thirty-four cyclists, aged between twenty-six and sixty-nine, from twenty-six Federations completed a 'Cycle Cuba' event during which they covered 350km and raised £85,000.

Denman is one of the many jewels in the WI crown, and it is highly valued; but it is an expensive resource to maintain and efforts to keep it going are unceasing.

Right from the start, the WI knew that financing their college would be a challenge …

BUILDINGS AND GROUNDS

Set back from the centre of Marcham, right next to All Saints' parish church, Denman immediately conveys an atmosphere of secluded elegance. The pineapples on the entrance gateposts have for centuries been a universal symbol of welcome and hospitality, and the short drive down to the house opens up into a splendid vista of parkland and magnificent trees. When the WI bought the estate, the grounds stretched to some 100 acres, but much of that has been sold off; the College now has seventeen acres of land. The modern houses to be seen peeping over the wall at the end of the long lawn in front of the house were built on the old walled market gardens, which were sold in the 1970s. Some of the other land was bought back by the Duffield family, who had sold the estate in 1938, but they have continued to allow access for rambles and country walks.

The main house

Lady Brunner had set out her vision of how the College would work day to day in her speech to the 1945 AGM. It was to be 'a traditional country house, with smallholding and garden attached, from which the College could be supplied with farm, garden and dairy produce'. The rooms would be full of the homely handicrafts for which the WI was famous. Yet despite the grandeur of the main house, early residents experienced rather a Spartan existence. When the College opened in 1948 there were beds in the house for thirty-one students: five single rooms, seven double rooms and four three-bedders. It was very much a 'dormitory life', and the lavatory and washing facilities were for some time quite inadequate when the College was full. Accommodation in the house is still available for students, including what were once servants' bedrooms on the top floor that have been converted into comfortable, if small, rooms. The windows here, however, were designed to prevent the servants from overlooking their employers' activities in the grounds below, so don't offer much in the way of a view. Most of the rooms are furnished with double beds, but several of those on the first floor can be shared and are supplied with two or three single beds; en suite bathrooms are the norm. From the beginning, most of the bedrooms have been sponsored by County Federations, so they all vary in the style of their furnishings and fabrics; the aim is to display and champion local arts and crafts. Yorkshire, for example, sponsored a triple bedroom at the start, and still has the same today; some of the furniture in the room is by Robert 'Mouseman' Thompson who lived and worked in Kilburn, North Yorkshire, and whose wooden furniture and artefacts, always adorned with a small mouse, are highly collectable.

Buildings and grounds

Hoeing vegetables in the
walled garden, 1950s.

Left Early visitors viewing the College before it was opened, 1940s.

Above The main house seen across the lake, 1991.

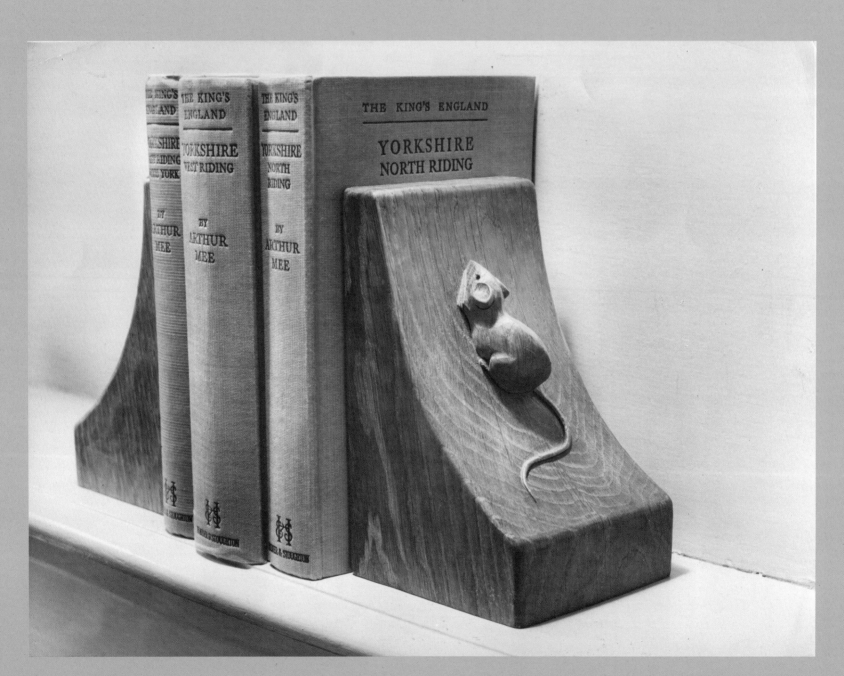

The public rooms in the main house deliberately retain the 'country house' feel that Lady Brunner and the members of the founding committee wanted. It was meant to be 'a big house of our own' and that was how its layout and furnishing were approached. The Drawing Room is a case in point; large and comfortable, with sofas and armchairs in abundance, its huge windows offer a splendid view of the parkland and grounds.

When the WI took Denman over from the Air Ministry, the room now to the right of the main door, known as the Livingstone Room, had been used as an operations room and had a low false ceiling. There had never been windows in that room to the front of the building, though symmetry was achieved on the outside by false stonework. In the 1980s, when rewiring work was being done, the false ceiling was removed to expose splendid plasterwork above, which was then restored, and at the same time the decision was taken to open up the windows. The room had been named for Sir Richard Livingstone in 1962, two years after his death; his seminal role in the foundation of the College is also recognised by a bronze bust of him, by Kathleen Parbury, which is to be found outside the north wall of the house; it is inscribed in Greek with the words 'lover of culture'.

Jean Varnam, then a NFWI Vice-Chairman, responsible while others were on holiday for the building work being carried out at Denman, recalled the discovery of the ceiling:

'One Saturday morning, I received an urgent call from David Austin, the Bursar. The workmen had removed the lights from the suspended ceiling and found, in almost perfect condition, the most beautiful carved ceiling. They wanted permission to remove the suspended ceiling and reveal the original one. I went to the College the next day and climbed the scaffolding, put my head through one of the light sockets and with a torch and a hard hat viewed what had been covered over for forty years. I could find no one to consult and as the workmen had to proceed on Monday morning, I took the decision to remove the suspended ceiling and bring in an expert from London to assess the damage and estimate the cost of repair. Having thrown all to the wind with the ceiling, I also asked whether they could uncover the fireplace – yet another gem – and I persuaded Wedgwood to give us the lovely vases which now grace it.'

Another splendid room is that named for John and Lil Nugent Harris, who were among those who helped Madge Watt in her determined efforts in 1913 to transplant the Canadian WI initiative to Britain. The Nugent Harris portraits hang on either side of the main door into the room; and the College has in its archives a splendid book presented to

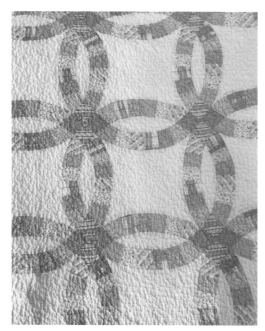

Above The bedspread in the Indiana Room, and a detail of it.

Right and opposite An example of the exquisite work traditionally put into the furnishings of rooms sponsored by County Federations.

EVEREST 1953   HALL GREEN W.I.

OLTON

11/8 TOTAL ECLIPSE 1999

Channel Tunnel 1994

BERKSWELL

ROYAL YACHT
BRITANNIA

LAST
VOYAGE
1997

HEART OF ENGLAND W.I.

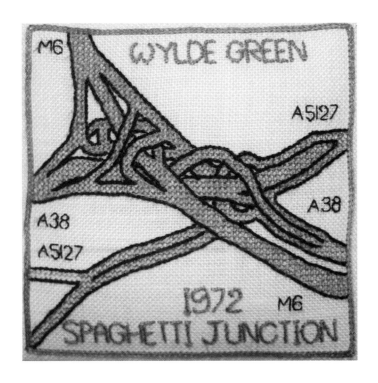

WYLDE GREEN

M6

A5127

A38

A38

A5127

1972

M6

SPAGHETTI JUNCTION

5

5 8 71 CHAY BLYTH SAILS
ROUND THE WORLD IN
YACHT BRITISH STEEL

GREAT BARR W I

HURST
GREEN

HALLEY'S COMET
1986

AUSTIN-MINI

1959

ALEC ISSIGONIS

£450

848 cc

MINI

SHIRLEY WI

Previous page Details
from the embroidered
panels which adorn
the West Midlands
bedroom.

Above A student
at the piano in the
Drawing Room, under
the portrait of Lady
Brunner.

Opposite Students using
the library, 1957.

John Nugent Harris in recognition of his long service to the Agricultural Organisation Society. The room – thought to be the oldest in the house – is now used mainly for meetings and administration; though it is also used as a sitting room by the tutors and is sometimes pressed into service as a small dining room, either as overspill when the College is bursting at the seams or when there are only a few students left at the end of a busy week. The dining room itself – called the Lady Denman Restaurant – had been built originally as an extension at the back of the house and was enlarged in the mid-1950s, with the work paid for from a fund set up in memory of Lady Denman after her death in 1954. With its big windows overlooking the grounds and its communal tables, it is a friendly space where students who are on their own can sit anywhere and be sure of a welcome and a chat with others on the table.

Next to the Nugent Harris Room is what is now the bar, a small room that started off as the Grace Hadow Library and still has a few books, though most are kept in the Teaching Centre. In the 1960s, after a licence had been obtained, alcohol could be bought from a tea trolley wheeled out to the front of the stairs in the evening. The bar, which replaced the drinks trolley and the library in 1988, now has quite the atmosphere of a private club where residents can enjoy a drink before dinner in the evenings, often spilling over into the Drawing Room next door. It may be that the founders would regret the demise of the library, for which Reynolds Stone designed elegant book plates; but there can be no doubt that the bar, with its tea and coffee facilities, its pile of games there to be borrowed and its deep leather armchairs add a great deal to the 'country house' feel of Denman.

The first floor is reached by an elegant staircase, one of the few relics of the pre-war tenure of Geoffrey Berners, who transplanted it here from a grand house in London. It used to lead to a spacious landing, but health and safety considerations in the 1980s led to it being screened off. It is still an attractive space, and is adorned with portraits of many of the women and men who were important to the history both of the WI and of the College. Residential rooms lead off the landing, including the Chairman's Room always allocated to the host, and stairs lead up to the smaller rooms on the top floor, once servants' bedrooms but now part of the overall accommodation.

The residential buildings

In 1949, the stables – renamed The Croft – were converted to provide nine more bedrooms for sixteen occupants. This arrangement lasted until 1953 when the building became used for staff flats and storage; it

Opposite left New Croft is seen in the foreground; Old Croft in the background, late 1950s. These are now replaced by Maple and Holly cottages.

Opposite right The dining room, 1957.

Above Students preparing vegetables in the Home Acres kitchen, 1952.

The Country Housewife Mural

Hanging in Studio 1 in the Teaching Centre until February 2009, the Mural – or Muriel, as the staff familiarly called it – was designed for the Festival of Britain in 1951 by Constance Howard, textile professor at Goldsmiths in London. Her students took six months to complete it, using many different embroidery techniques such as collage, blackwork and stump work; one of the students, reputed to have made the red and white striped blouse on the table in the middle of the picture, was Mary Quant, and much of the miniature craftwork featured in the piece came from WI members. After the festival, the mural was given to Denman. In recent years, it began to deteriorate badly and needed conservation, but the funds could not be found to do the work. It was therefore decided that it should be handed over to the National Needlework Archive, where it was initially exposed to dry nitrogen treatment to kill off any pests. It has now been restored by students at the Royal College of Needlework and will remain at the National Needlework Archive in Newbury.

was demolished in 1961. New Croft had replaced it in 1953, offering eighteen single rooms and surviving until 1997.

In the mid-1960s, thoughts began to turn to new buildings, for both accommodation and teaching. Berkshire County Council had decided not to renew its lease on Home Acres (see p108) and the teaching huts were anyway coming to the end of their lives. There were worries that the Institutes might not look too kindly on yet another fundraising campaign. But then came a windfall: early in 1966, the College received a munificent anonymous gift of £30,000 towards the cost of new buildings, given to ensure that they would be of a standard befitting the College. Plans were drawn up for both a new teaching centre and a residential block, and in spring 1968 contractors moved onto the site between the main house and New Croft where the buildings would be situated. As work proceeded, it became clear that the plans were too ambitious for the money available, but Sir Felix and Lady Brunner stepped into the breach and guaranteed the extra funds. The buildings opened in 1970.

The design of both buildings was innovative and ahead of its time, centring as it did on a series of hexagonal rooms. The two-storied residential block incorporated a flat for the Bursar and accommodation for two other staff; that part of the building was later handed over to the twelve Welsh Federations to turn into two bedrooms, and is now

called Gwalia, the ancient name for Wales. The rest of the building was named for the Brunners; it is now divided into Brunner 2 and Brunner 3.

The striking design was not, however, entirely successful in that rainwater drainage was carried down within the structure, resulting in continuous problems with leaks and damp. The rooms could also get very hot in summer; Helen Anderson recalled that a class of potters in the Bawden Studio were to be found with their feet in bowls of cold water during the unusually hot summer of 1976. Repair works were carried out in the mid-1980s, and the later residential buildings benefited from the lessons learned.

The other residential blocks that followed in that part of the grounds all offer attractive, comfortable rooms with en suite bathrooms, each one as ever sponsored and maintained by one of the County Federations, and some of them containing rooms designed for disabled students and their carers. Built between 1979 and 1997, they are called Holly, Willow, Maple, Oak and Beech; and there are other buildings in the area used for a variety of purposes, one as the NFWI Unit, converted out of Jasmine Cottage in 1996 for use as the base of the NFWI Craft and Training departments. Christmas Cottage remained as the Warden's residence until the retirement of Hilda Jones, and was then used as accommodation for staff who had to stay overnight, as

well as occasionally for tutors and even students. Later Principals lived in one of the two thatched cottages in the grounds, which have also been used for tutors when the College is full.

Teaching facilities

The first teaching facilities were in the main house, where the spacious rooms on the ground floor could be used for both lectures and practical work, though the house could accommodate only a small demonstration kitchen for cookery courses. The large garage was pressed into use for pursuits such as pottery; a letter from a Surrey member recalled that 'We were not allowed in the College for mid-morning coffee or afternoon tea, it was brought out to us [in the garage]. Dirty? We were filthy!' The garage was also used for the messy parts of the cookery classes, such as demonstrating the butchering of half a pig. But very soon the extra accommodation provided by the bedrooms in The Croft meant that the demonstration kitchen had to be sacrificed to allow more dining room space, so a caravan contributed by the Kent Federation, which was fitted up as a canteen, became an interim demonstration facility.

Clearly, the huts left in the grounds by the Air Ministry could be useful, but their conversion into effective teaching accommodation would be costly. By a happy chance, however, Berkshire County Council

was looking for a site for a new Rural Domestic Economy School, and it was suggested that it might join forces with the WI at Denman. The County Council was offered a lease on two of the huts and some of the land, and the two bodies each contributed half of the costs needed to convert the huts into a demonstration centre, to be named Home Acres. This successful collaboration between the WI and the County Council lasted until 1967 when Berkshire moved its centre to the new Further Education College at Abingdon.

A small booklet published by the Berkshire Agricultural Education Committee (undated but certainly from the 1950s) gave a list of lectures, demonstrations and courses in horticulture, rural domestic economy, dairying, small livestock and bee-keeping available to WIs, village produce associations, horticultural societies and other organisations within the county. The section on Home Acres pointed out that 'This development takes place at a time when the economical use of food has assumed great importance in the national economy, and it is hoped that housewives will make full use of the centre … The facilities are intended for all sections of the community in Berkshire but will make a special appeal to those living in the north of the county. In this district, cut off from the activities centred round Reading, lies the most rural part of Berkshire. The centre is the first of

Opposite The new
Teaching Centre.

Above Thelma Jones
demonstrating how to
cut up chops to a group
of students, 1949.

Royal opening ceremonies

Left The Queen Mother being presented with a bouquet by Lady Brunner's granddaughter, with Lady Brunner immediately behind.

Opposite The Queen Mother arriving to open the Teaching Centre.

Her Majesty Queen Elizabeth The Queen Mother visited Denman on 4 April 1970 to perform the opening ceremonies for Brunner House and the Teaching Centre. Helen Anderson was Warden at the time, and recalled the occasion during a taped interview in the early 1990s. 'The opening was due to take place in the area between Brunner and the Teaching Centre, where we built an official stand. When we woke at about 6am on the day, there was deep snow everywhere. We hesitated about moving to our wet weather alternative in the hope that it might thaw by midday – and miraculously it did. But then, just after Her Majesty had arrived and just before the ceremony was due to begin, we got a phone call to say that a bomb may have been planted in Brunner House. There were police everywhere, who were very tactful but left rather a lot of muddy footprints all over the house. No bomb was found!

'Her Majesty was so friendly and easy with everyone. Sylvia Grey, then NFWI Chairman, hoped that she wouldn't be too cold, and she replied: Oh, don't worry about that, I always wear plenty of winter woollies underneath.' She also said: 'I do wish I'd had the chance to come on a course.' There was lots of jockeying for position on the dais with Her Majesty.

'That whole week was set aside for visits from WIs all over the country. We had coachload after coachload of people pouring through the gates, and we had a huge marquee in the garden with non-stop catering going on. One of the days was set aside for the education authorities to whom we wanted to show off our new facilities. By the end of the week, all the staff were totally exhausted – Sylvia Grey came again on the Saturday to make sure we were still alive!'

The expansion of the Teaching Centre to accommodate a new Home Economics Centre came when Hilda Jones was Principal. Work began on it in May 1978, and, as she later recalled: 'We decided to ask Her Majesty The Queen whether she would agree to open it. It took until just before Christmas for the palace to say yes, and even then we weren't allowed to announce it until the next gazette appeared after Christmas. However, I was allowed to tell the staff at the Christmas party that she would pay what was called an informal visit to the College in April to perform the opening ceremony.

'I was never quite sure afterwards what "informal" meant. There was so much pressure, so much organisation, so many discussions! I was visited every week of those three months by the Queen's private secretary, the Lord Lieutenant of Oxfordshire, the Chief Constable, the Press Association – they all came again and again. The Queen's chauffeur came twice to make sure of the route. And then terrible weather in January put the programme back by three weeks. All the contractors insisted that completion by April 9 would

be impossible – except that the Queen was coming! A lorry strike didn't help either. We had to plan the marquee, the car parking, the flowers, the catering. It was meant to be informal, but the security was frightening.

'Then we had to consider whom to invite. We decided to offer places to two representatives from each County Federation, to many of the lecturers who'd been coming to the College for a while, to the whole of the WI hierarchy, and to our voluntary helpers. There was not one refusal. Moreover, the Queen was coming during an ordinary working week when courses would be going on, and as usual we'd overbooked some of the courses because there were always cancellations. But, of course, on this occasion no one would be likely to cancel, so we booked extra beds in the village.

'We were asked if we wanted the Royal Standard to fly on the day; it arrived in a cylindrical packet which the postman, for some reason, thought was loo paper for Her Majesty! We raised it on the flagpole in the grounds but there was not a breath of wind on the day so, sadly, no one saw it.

'There was a lot of generosity. We wrote to all the major home equipment firms asking for donations for the new centre and telling them that the Queen would be opening it. We got an instantaneous response; gifts poured in between January and March, some of them, I have to say, useless, but all very generous. One came from a local firm whom we had asked to replace our very shabby front hall carpet at, we hoped, a discount; they gave it to us free, provided we photographed the Queen standing on it. As the day approached, Jersey sent us 300 carnations, which had to be collected from the port because of a strike; one of our helpful WI husbands did that for us, and because they had had to be sent early to be sure of arriving on time, Jersey also sent a generous cheque to buy fizzy lemonade to put them in so that they would last.

'The week before the royal visit I was on Woman's Hour with Sue MacGregor, and was scared I'd make a hash of it while WI members from all over the country would be listening in. But it all went well, and I was thrilled when Her Majesty told me that she'd heard it. A last-minute glitch came when we were told that the Queen always keeps the scissors with which she cuts ribbons, and replaces them with a silver coin in a commemorative case; but we had borrowed a beautiful gold pair from Lady Brunner, so we had to tell the palace that they were not ours to give away. On the day, Her Majesty handed them back to me with a twinkle in her eye; and we still got the commemorative coin (now in the archives).

'April 9 was a rather dull day. We had sniffer dogs all over the place and we were afraid that the flowers would be frozen as it was so cold. All went well. Her Majesty opened the centre, visited the Norfolk Room, and popped into a rose-growing course – where she disagreed with the tutor who was recommending pruning in March whereas she thought January was better. She had tea in the marquee, and I presented her with an engraved glass bowl made by Brian Feden, one of our tutors, who also engraved the plaque on the centre. And she stayed till 5 o'clock.'

....

Miss Elaine Lewis and myself were lucky enough to be allocated the two executive tickets to this event for our County Federation. After the Queen Mother opened the new Brunner House, she was shown round it while we waited outside, and got ourselves as near to her Rolls-Royce as we could. The chauffeur was standing beside it, and Miss Lewis started talking to him – and it transpired that he was from Pembroke Dock and Miss Lewis had taught his aunt at Aberaeron School. He opened the rear door and let us see where the Queen Mother sat with extra cushions behind her and in front of her seat a little velvet-covered cupboard containing a silver flask of brandy and a little casket of biscuits to keep her going on the journey. Later, the Queen Mother came over and she was suddenly face to face with us. Given a prod, I managed a hurried curtsey. **Evelyn Gibbings, Rhydlewis WI**

....

Left (l–r) Helen Anderson, Sylvia Grey and the Queen Mother, who is about to sign the visitors' book.

Below left The Queen signing the visitors' book, with NFWI Chairman Patricia Batty Shaw.

Below right The Queen being introduced to Hilda Jones (Principal), Anne Ballard (NFWI General Secretary), Kate Foss (Treasurer) and Vera Drew (Vice-Chairman).

A gardening course in the
old walled garden, 1954.

its kind to be devoted entirely to the production, costing, marketing and utilisation of home-grown food, and its development will be watched with great interest.'

The premises provided a demonstration kitchen with room for twelve to fifteen students with electric, Calor gas, oil and solid fuel cooking stoves, a model home kitchen to be used for practical demonstrations and exhibits, a preservation kitchen equipped for fruit canning, bacon curing and soft cheese making, and a facility for some of the horticultural and bee-keeping processes. There was also a garden for the cultivation of fruit, flowers and vegetables, an allotment for growing vegetables, mainly for marketing, a paddock for small livestock on a domestic scale – pigs for bacon, poultry, rabbits, bees and goats – and an allotment for growing supplementary food for livestock.

In 1970, when the Teaching Centre was opened, Home Acres was demolished. The new building, single-storied with hexagonal rooms lit by central lanterns, initially provided four studios: one for heavy craft such as pottery and upholstery, named after Charlotte Bawden; one for all kinds of textile work; and two used for other courses such as painting and, in recent years, computer work. It contained a small preparation kitchen and two cookers that could be used for demonstrations, but there was still no room for practical cookery; students on such courses had to be taken to the college in Abingdon, which was not the most convenient of arrangements. And there were some teething problems. A peculiar smell in the Bawden studio turned out to be sewage backing up because a workman had left a plank in the sewage pipes. When it was removed, the workmen were nearly drowned in sewage! And for some while, the innovative hexagonal roofs leaked.

Denman was finally able to offer fully practical cookery courses when the Home Economics Centre was added to the Teaching Centre in 1979. This new facility, with fully equipped demonstration and practical kitchen, allowed a vast expansion in the range of courses that could be accommodated, and offered the opportunity to embrace new and specialist ventures. Subsequent building work has involved extending the foyer in 1991, and the addition of the Ferris Room, a large, light room with a sprung floor for dancing.

The grounds

When the NFWI bought Marcham Park, the grounds extended to about 100 acres of parkland. It is likely that they were initially laid out in the early nineteenth century by Emily and Thomas Duffield who, along with their Duffield successors, probably planted at least some of the sixty species of tree that still glorify the park – among them the giant

Far left Sylvia Grey, the Queen Mother and a swan.

Left The lake in the 1950s.

Repair and maintenance

For the first forty years of its history, because of the NFWI's determination to keep the fees as low as possible, the repair and maintenance of the buildings had been a low priority. By the mid-1980s, there was therefore a backlog of work that needed doing, and this coincided with the introduction of new fire regulations for public buildings. In the main house, the roofs, chimneys and the electrical system were in a sadly neglected state, and there was a problem with damp. But even more urgent and expensive was the work needed to bring the estate up to standard in terms of the fire regulations. Second staircases were required in New Croft and on the top floor of the main house, a firebreak had to be inserted on the first floor, and emergency lighting had to be installed throughout. The fire officer told the College that unless the work was put in hand immediately he would have no option other than to close it down.

The Trustees had to consider seriously whether the money needed – half a million pounds – could be raised and whether the College was in fact viable. Their consultant was pessimistic. But the Federations consulted their members and voted overwhelmingly to save the College and to start an appeal for a million pounds, half of which would fund the work and the other half go to boost the endowment reserve. The launch of the appeal allowed funds to be released immediately so that work could start in September 1986 when the College was closed for four weeks; and the appeal target was reached within an astonishing two years.

Major building work taking place on the first-floor landing as the main house is completely rewired in the 1980s.

<u>DENMAN COLLEGE</u>

<u>Gardening All the Year Round Course.</u>

<u>April 11th - 14th 1949.</u>

Chairman - Miss Sandars.

MONDAY 11th.	4.45 p.m.	<u>Talk.</u> How to make the most of the Garden, including a tour of the garden, with questions. Miss Clarke .
	8 p.m.	Welcome and Talk on Denman College. Miss Christmas.
TUESDAY 12th	9.30 - 11	<u>Demonstration.</u> Tools - usual and unusual; when and how to use them. Miss Clarke
	11.15 - 12.45	<u>Talk.</u> Cropping Plan - The Seed List. Miss Clarke
		Afternoon free.
	5 - 6 p.m.	<u>Practical.</u> Demonstration of Growing Soft Fruit. Miss Clarke & Mr. Barnes.
	6 - 6.30	Pruning of Fruit Trees. Miss Clarke & Mr. Barnes.
	8 p.m.	Community Singing, with a short Talk on Music. Mrs. Archer.
WEDNESDAY 13th	9.30-10.45	<u>Talk.</u> a) Manures & the Compost Heap. b) Pests & Diseases. Miss Clarke & Mr. Barnes.
	11.15 - 12.45	<u>Practical</u> Seed Sowing Pricking Out Transplanting. Miss Clarke & Mr. Barnes.

Afternoon. Visit to Blenheim Palace Gardens.

	8 p.m.	Film and talk on Garden Birds. Mr. Smallcombe.
THURSDAY 14th	9.30-10.45	<u>Demonstration & Practical.</u> Students' Requests. Miss Clarke & Mr. Barnes.
	11.15-12.45	<u>Talk.</u> Flowers, including the Rock Garden & the Herbaceous Border. Mr. Danks.
	12.45	Lunch.

Students leave after lunch.

Sequoia Wellingtonias, which were introduced and planted throughout the country after the death of Wellington in 1861. The goldfish pond is late nineteenth century in date, and the lake was enlarged in the 1930s.

An early priority for the new NFWI owners was dealing with the poor state into which the park had fallen during the tenure of the Air Ministry. Mary Clarke, the gardener and one of the first new members of staff, set about clearing out excess trees and shrubs, mending fences and replanting the thirty-two acres of woodland. The lake was restored, and two pairs of swans arrived in 1949, the gift of the Keeper of the King's Swans, though the College had to pay £5 3s 11d for catching and transporting them. Although the first pair turned out to be rather aggressive and had to be replaced, swans remained happily on the lake for decades, and indeed provided the first – and so far, the only – births at the College. Hilda Jones was able to announce to the AGM of 1978 that three cygnets had been born – promptly named A(ndrew), G(eorge), and M(egan). The swans had departed by the late 1990s, but were for a time replaced by a peacock, which turned up unbidden and kept students awake with its screams.

Madge Watt died in 1948, and the following spring an avenue of 300 lime trees was planted at Denman in her memory. Some thirty years later, the avenue was becoming overcrowded, so every other tree was uprooted and sold off as an 'instant tree' for £50 – rather an advance on the £1 each that they had initially cost. A large herb garden surrounded by a beech hedge was an early addition, along with an attractive herbaceous border 100 metres long backed by a south-facing wall and complemented by a scented garden. And in 1970, a woodland path was opened up through the Warren which ran around the perimeter of the estate and was laid out as a nature trail with the help of Judy Poor of the Oxford Federation, whose husband was a professor of forestry. This is now on the land sold back to the Duffield family in the 1970s, but access is still allowed to Denman students.

The walled market garden, which had been regarded as such a valuable addition to the facilities when the estate was first bought, indeed proved its worth during the first couple of years. An apple and pear orchard, a large area planted with soft fruit, and a flourishing vegetable garden provided for all the College's needs as well as giving a surplus that was sold off profitably. But by the early 1950s it was becoming less viable, and was let, with a cottage, to a tenant. During that decade, the livestock were also disposed of. Twenty years later, as Helen Anderson recalled: 'It was becoming clear that the four acres of kitchen garden and the glass houses were going to wrack and ruin under the tenancy, and so we decided to sell. We picked the last harvest of marvellous fruit that

Opposite The itinerary for the Gardening All the Year Round course, 1949.

Right Lime Tree Walk, 2000.

Gardeners and groundsmen

Peter Lawrence was the gardener at Denman from 24 September 1973 to 24 January 1995, when he retired. He compiled a magnificent album, now in the archives, with press cuttings, a timeline of the building's history, and scores of photographs documenting the building work, the events and courses, the special occasions, and the gardens themselves during his twenty-two years at Denman. He wrote at the end of the album: 'I would like to add my postscript for the benefit of all future gardeners: I believe in letting nature look after itself – with just a little help, nature will achieve its own balance. Especially if you are virtually single-handed for the first fifteen years!'

Peter Lawrence setting about cultivating herbaceous plants as part of a WI campaign, 1980s.

Betty Christmas, dogs and a visitor enjoying the flowers bordering the walled kitchen gardens (now the Farthings).

went around the high walls with great sadness. We got rid of the tenants who were running the garden and converted their cottage into student accommodation for a while.'

The sale yielded £118,000, which was put into an endowment fund for the Home Economics Centre, and the land was used for a new estate of houses. Miss Anderson also recalled her sadness when the gales of 1976 knocked down several of the big old trees that were such an ornament to the park.

The estate as a whole was becoming more burdensome to maintain by this time, and it was the Duffield family who came to the rescue when John Duffield offered to buy the seventy-seven acres of land round the College at a price per acre well above the going rate. He would also restore the perimeter walls, which had become almost impossible to keep in repair, would look after the woodland, and would still allow the College access to Lime Tree Walk and the nature trail. The sale went ahead for £167,000 plus the maintenance costs, with the money put into a fund for future maintenance. 'It was a great ending to my twenty years at the College,' said Hilda Jones.

The work of the gardeners and groundsmen has frequently been lightened by members who maintain and develop different sections of the gardens; occasionally the husband of a WI member who is on a course will come with her to lend a hand in the garden. The grounds are often used in summer for art courses and for other activities that require space and open air. Hilda Jones again: 'I introduced archery courses, but realised the hazards when they took place at the same time as courses in the herb garden.' Even though diminished in size from the 100 acres when the College opened, the estate is still a happy hunting ground for naturalists and gardeners, whether or not as part of a formal course. And, of course, they provide a tranquil setting for those who want a gentle stroll or just to sit and commune with nature.

....

I heard about Denman in 1948, the year I took my last post as headmistress of a small village school. I had never heard of the WI, having always worked in a city. A week after I started school, my furniture arrived – and I was also awaiting the arrival of my elderly parents and had no idea how I was going to find the time to take them for a meal. At this point two ladies carrying large baskets walked into school. One said, 'Good morning Miss Rippon, we are members of the Women's Institute. We know you are expecting your parents today and will have difficulties feeding them … so would you like to let us loose in your kitchen?' Can you wonder that I loved them on the spot and have adored the WI ever since?

I did not manage to get to Denman until I was seventy-nine. I was a little apprehensive, but needlessly; the moment I entered the College I felt welcome and immediately fell under Denman's magic spell. On one visit for a painting course in brilliant August weather, we were turned out into the grounds, me with my temperamental easel, to paint a picture. I managed the background of bushes and rushes, but a glorious tall tree was less successful – in fact I don't think I've ever seen a better stick of rhubarb! After lunch it looked no better – and then the easel fell over, depositing my painting face down in the grass. I was about to tear it up in disgust when the tutor came over and put it back on the easel. We both looked at it and giggled. The grass had done what I couldn't. It had smudged the stick of rhubarb into quite a presentable tree, and the blades of grass all over my lake made it look most realistic, almost a collage. So my effort went up on the wall.

If young, middle-aged ladies and old ladies like me can enjoy going to Denman, then there must be something there for every member.

Elsie Rippon, writing in the early 1990s at the age of eighty-seven
....

Left A painting class, 2000s.

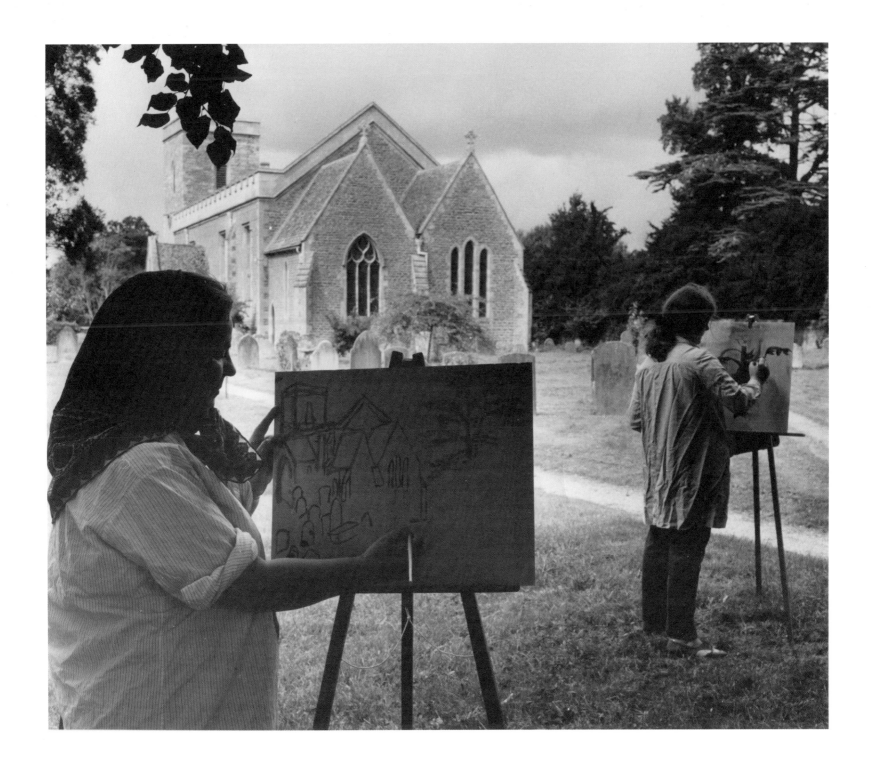

Above Students painting
in All Saints' churchyard,
1969.

Overleaf A watercolour
course in the College
grounds, 1980s.

LIVING AND LEARNING AT DENMAN

It is only within the last few years that students at Denman have not been expected to lend a hand with domestic chores during their stay. At the beginning, they were all on a rota to help with washing up, and had to make their beds, mop out their rooms and change their sheets on departure. In the dining hall, the woman sitting at the end of the table acted as 'mum', dishing out the food and collecting the plates at the end of the meal. It was noteworthy that Denman regulars tended to avoid that particular seat.

Lady Brunner was sure that the students would be more than willing to help out with domestic chores so that costs could be kept down: 'No member would feel it unreasonable to carry out a rota of household jobs for an hour in the morning, with occasional turns at washing-up and laying meals.' Not everyone who attended, however, was so keen; and when it became clear in the mid-1950s that the dining and kitchen arrangements were inadequate, there was near-universal relief that the provision of a 'washing-up machine' now meant that washing up rotas for students could be abandoned.

As Ruth Fenney (Glenfield WI, Leics) remembers: 'Staying at Denman was very different in the 1970s. Then, students were expected to change their own beds on departure, and were supplied with tea towels as part of the linen in the room so that they could wash up their own tea cups. There were no locks on the doors of the rooms, though this changed when there was increased pressure to open up Denman to non-WI members and also as a bed and breakfast facility.'

Although residents are no longer expected to change their sheets on departure, they still tend to make their own beds and return their dishes to the serving hatch at the end of breakfast and lunch. So staying at Denman is not quite the same as staying at a hotel – not least perhaps because the rooms are not provided with televisions. Whether or not to do so has been the subject of debate, but the consensus is still firmly on the side of the status quo – though the provision of wifi throughout the College now allows media access to those who want it.

Until 1985, the College employed resident kitchen staff, but at that point the catering was put out to external contractors, as has been the case ever since. The food is of a high standard: breakfast offers the full English for those who want it, plus fruit, cereals, fruit juices and toast, all served as a buffet; lunch is a buffet too, with a choice of hot meals as well as salad and puddings; and supper is served by waiters from a three-course menu offering three choices per course. Coffee and tea in the mid-morning and mid-afternoon breaks are self-service from the bar in the main house and wheeled out to the Teaching Centre, accompanied by cakes and biscuits. Food

Right The Worcestershire bedroom, 2000s.

Far right The Guernsey bedroom, 1950s.

Living and learning at Denman

Above The
Northumberland
bedroom, 1950s.

preferences are catered for: there are always vegetarian and gluten-free options. The bar is open before and after dinner for those who want a soft or alcoholic drink, though some courses have sessions in the evening, so those students do not linger after dinner – though they may come back later to relax in the Drawing Room or the bar over a further drink and a chat.

Hilda Jones recalled some of those who needed special care. 'There was a woman with anorexia whose husband said that she might manage a boiled egg over the weekend but that we should just let her sit and talk to people. Her weekend was a great success and she came back twice, partly for the marvellous comfort of being here. We had a miscarriage and a death and many heart attacks, but no births apart from the cygnets (see p119). There was an epileptic seizure during dinner, and a bee stung someone who was allergic and nearly died – but the doctor came within ten minutes, as he so often did, and she was fine. One woman, who had been persuaded by a friend to come on a painting course, lost courage completely on her first evening, shut herself in her room, and insisted that she wouldn't be able to compete and would pack up and go immediately. After much argument, she was persuaded to change her mind, and turned out to be much the most gifted student on the course.'

The friendship, camaraderie, challenge and stimulus found at Denman provide support and comfort too. A student on a writing course in the mid-1980s realised, along with the rest of her class, that there were six widows among them: 'One was bravely facing her first outing since her loss, others were still finding it tough going, two were further along the recovery process. Something occurred during our time together that week which bonded us in a way that continued. We write a letter or share a piece of writing and send it round the circle. Some visit or phone each other. Our writing skills were challenged that week and we moved on in other ways too.'

As part of the College's aim to broaden horizons in the early days, entertainment – with more than a touch of educational relevance – was provided on Thursday evenings at the end of the last day of the course. A regular then was Margaret Deneke, sister of Helena Deneke, biographer of Grace Hadow, who gave piano recitals, and was sometimes accompanied by her sister who sang; both would dress up in evening clothes and jewellery to make the occasion more special. When Helen Anderson was Warden, she often gave song recitals and told stories about her time in the chorus at Glyndebourne. Sometimes there were talks on foreign countries, at a time when few travelled abroad.

Opposite **Students eating their evening meal, 1950s.**

Right **The Wiltshire bedroom.**

Later, the entertainment tended to reflect the courses held that week; a music course, or one on country dancing, would result in its students demonstrating what they had learned, and those who had been studying the 1920s would throw a party with appropriate costumes. Today, music or dance courses often end with a mini-show put on by the class for fellow-students and staff. Jean York, from Gamlingay (Cambridge) WI, has visited Denman about twenty times over the past twelve years, mostly doing patchwork and other craft courses, and has come more frequently since she lost her husband a few years ago. She is sometimes accompanied by a friend, but is also quite happy to come on her own because, as she says, 'I feel quite safe and totally welcome here'.

She has also been once for the New Year party, and will certainly come again when her new puppy is more settled. She came in 2016 with three friends from her Federation, and had a wonderful time over three days and nights from their arrival on 30 December. They went to the pantomime in Oxford, had a trip to a museum, and enjoyed a ceilidh, live music, a seasonal quiz, and a full seven-course meal on New Year's Eve. There were workshops offering various craft courses, and they saw the New Year in with fireworks on the television. And afterwards, she said, 'I went out into the grounds and it was magically frosty.' The College was full, mainly of single people

Arriving for a ukulele course, I was lifting my ukulele, in its black case, from my car. 'That looks interesting,' said a lady who had parked next to me. 'Where do they set up the targets? On the lawn?' It took a moment for me to realise that she thought I had a gun in the case! No thought that I might have been a terrorist then? By the time I had gathered my thoughts she had moved on. She must have thought we had an extremely well silenced course that weekend! Might be an idea for a course actually – but ukulele is more fun.
Jean Emes, Royston Afternoon WI

who might otherwise have been on their own over the New Year. 'Denman at its best.'

Ruth Fenney has been to Denman getting on for eighty times on courses and also as host, which she does two or three times a year. She has been a WI member since 1971, and first came to Denman in 1976 for Making the Most of Your Sewing Machine. She serviced her own car during a car maintenance course, and did a great deal of choral singing in the 1990s with Ronald Allen Smith, then the WI's Music Adviser. She has gone on rambling and music appreciation courses, but in the last few years has concentrated on craft. Her husband and daughter have also frequently been to Denman. She says that she has never not enjoyed a

Left and opposite WI members at Denman taking part in dramatic performances.

Demonstrating different
ways to curtsey at a
drama rehearsal, c.1960.

Special events

A garden party at
Denman, 1971.

Some 10,000 WI members were able to visit Denman in 1947 before its opening the following year, and ever since then the buildings and grounds have been used for special events and celebrations. These have had the main twin aims of enhancing Denman's profile and of encouraging new women to come; the raising of money has sometimes been a fruitful side effect.

The opening of new buildings and facilities has always been an excuse for a party – and when the Queen and the Queen Mother visited to open new facilities (see pp110–13), the opportunity was taken to surround the occasions with much jollification, and there was inevitably a great demand for invitations. Flower festivals in 1958 and 1987 were attended by thousands, the 1987 one designed to show members how the money raised in the Save Denman appeal was being spent. In 1992, 14,000 visitors came to two festivals, Focus on Europe and Autumn at Denman, when the exhibits, stalls and music spilled over into All Saints' next door.

The biggest celebration so far was in 1995 on the fiftieth anniversary of the decision to set up the College, when more than 900 WI members took part in *Denman Fanfare*, a musical specially commissioned from Colin Tarn, a popular music tutor, which was performed in a huge marquee on the lawn: three performances a day for the six days of the festival. Some 15,000 people saw the musical, and around the fringes there were poetry readings under the trees, music in the church, rounders matches in the evenings … Those taking part threw everything into the event and exhausted themselves, but felt privileged and proud to be part of it.

course; and when asked whether she has had any bad experiences at Denman remembers an occasion when she and her husband arrived to find that the main house had lost all its hot water. 'But the staff rose to the challenge, as they always do, and we were put into Christmas Cottage where we had a lovely time.' She remembers a heated debate about whether or not to supply televisions in the rooms. Many felt that this would spoil the experience of being at Denman and could also cause an issue with the noise levels in the bedrooms. So there remains the one television in the hall at Denman, which is switched on for the news or, very rarely, for important TV occasions like the last episode of *Poldark* or the *Strictly Come Dancing* final.

Above all, she feels that at the heart of Denman is the strong feeling of home, a family feeling that embraces staff, students, tutors and everyone who visits. The commitment of the staff and their close involvement with Denman regulars mean that they are sorely missed when they move on or are away. Every time she comes, she feels that she is back with old friends, and she both notices change and appreciates the things that don't change. She finds it difficult to understand why more WI members don't take advantage of the College or, even worse, don't see its point: 'What happens here ripples down to members everywhere. The number who attend each year may be a relatively small proportion of WI members generally. But new women come every year and those who come return. The secret is to tempt them here for the first time. Denman started with the aim of offering further learning opportunities to women who would never otherwise have had those chances. It still does that today.'

Anne Stamper is a member of the Ringmer Evening WI and has held a variety of positions in the WI both nationally and within her Federation. She has been a tutor and a student at Denman on countless occasions, and is now the archivist of the College. She remembers her

----

My parents moved to very rural west Dorset in 1949. My mother and I joined Blackdown WI three years later (I still have my membership card). I was one of four teenage members. An older member and I shared a bursary to Denman and I chose the Nature Study course ('wildlife' had not been invented then), much of which I remember well — rising early to hear the dawn chorus and studying chalk hill flora at the Uffington White Horse. At fourteen, I was the youngest member to stay at Denman before Mother and Daughter courses began. In later years, my husband and I between us enjoyed twenty-four different courses.
Jill Russell, Wiltshire (Associate Member)

An aerial view of Christmas Cottage, 1950s.

Photography classes have grown in popularity in recent years.

first visit: 'In 1968, as a relatively new member of the WI, I won a bursary. I did wonder how my husband would feel about being left to look after our children (one and four years old at the time), but he said they would be fine if it was just for a weekend, so I came on my first visit to Denman. I chose a course on twentieth-century writers; there were three linked courses on modern novelists, modern poets and modern dramatists, and I chose the dramatists. We were sent a list of pre-course reading – this was to be serious stuff – so I did my homework and arrived at Denman feeling a bit apprehensive. The course was stimulating; we had some joint sessions with the other courses when visiting lecturers (drawn in from Oxford) gave the broad picture, and the rest of the time was spent with our own tutor reading and discussing the plays we had read.

'I returned home wondering how the family had got on without me. I need not have worried. I was greeted by a small boy who hardly had time to say hello before he was telling me "Daddy made this lovely pudding!" I knew then that I could continue to leave my family from time to time to come to Denman, as I have done ever since in a variety of roles – as tutor, education adviser, archivist, but above all as student.'

As all old houses are incomplete without a ghost, Denman reputedly has one too, whose haunting centres on the Livingstone Room. Jill Gooch, of the Suffolk West Federation, decided to use the tale to enliven one evening of her course: 'I went quietly upstairs to my room (I was staying in the main house) and dressed up as the ghost. I put on a wig I had bought, pulled a sheet over my body, and took my shoes and tights off. As it was evening the stairs were quite dim, so I crept down, stopped on the first landing, and peered into the reception hall where people were sitting, and then flittered down and round the room. What a shock some people had – and a certain Federation (not mine) never spoke to me again during the whole course!'

....

I've been to Denman many times, have done various art courses and, now that I am a grandma and my children have persuaded me into using a digital camera, the Photography course was a must too! I also wanted to write my life story for my grandsons because their upbringing was going to be so different to mine. I was born in Tanganyika (now Tanzania) and had lots of stories to tell. But I wasn't getting very far, so the Write Your Life Story course felt like a lifeline. Chrissie Hall, our tutor, gave us all sorts to think about and some very useful writing exercises. I now go on two writing retreats a year with Chrissie, and am getting closer to my aim of making a scrapbook for my grandsons.

Jill Eldridge, Berinsfield (Oxon) WI

....

'I now go on two writing retreats a year with Chrissie, and am getting closer to my aim of making a scrapbook for my grandsons.'

Left The elegant eighteenth-century staircase, transplanted to Denman from a grand house in London by Geoffrey Berners.

For more than a century, the Women's Institutes have been at the heart of education for women who have lacked the opportunity to enjoy the fruits of further education and training, whether in the skills needed for daily life or in wider cultural and artistic pursuits. The vision and steeliness of those founder pioneers met a ready audience in the thousands who signed up to this new women's organisation as soon as it arrived in Britain from Canada. The clamour they raised for opportunities to learn, to mix with the like-minded, and to develop their brains and their knowledge astonished and galvanised the educational establishment. The WI's growth was speedy and phenomenal. Aimed originally at countrywomen, it later embraced urban women too, and its members were soon to come from every class of society and every level of attainment. The campaigns it has undertaken over the hundred years of its existence have been deeply influential in shaping society. As the *Observer* wrote of the WI in 1999: 'Let's try some word association. Women's Institutes: Bramble jelly, singing "Jerusalem", Victoria sponge cake? Wrong. Think eco-warriors, domestic violence, prostitution, third-world debt, child abuse, nude calendars, drugs.' As a highly successful and forceful voice for change, the WI is only ever underestimated by those who know nothing about it. And its beginnings had their roots firmly embedded in education.

Those roots have grown ever stronger and dug themselves ever deeper. The establishment of Denman in 1947 was the culmination of the hopes and aspirations not just of the WI itself but also of forward-thinking educationalists who knew that the broadening of access to learning was both desirable and inevitable. Denman is, and always has been, only part of the educational work that the WI undertakes, at both national and Federation levels – although it may be said to be at the heart of all that work. The WI's own College still thrives, still offers wonderful learning opportunities for WI members – and others – from everywhere in the country. The 'Denman experience' is enjoyed by thousands every year.

But Denman is much more than a beautiful place with splendid facilities. As its founders intended, it sends out ripples to Federations and individual WIs everywhere, stimulating women to seek out educational possibilities closer to home, and offering more and more distance learning. This is perhaps an increasing part of its future: to continue to provide a solid core of educational enterprise while offering a growing outreach facility everywhere that the WI has a presence.

Right Campaigning has always been at the heart of the WI. A delegation of WI members is seen here on their way to present a petition of 600,000 signatures to 10 Downing Street, 1954.

I have been a member of the WI for twenty-eight years, belonging to four different WIs around the country, and have been to Denman forty-four times so far. The best was in 1994 when I did an Advanced Driving Course, which ran from Monday evening to Friday lunchtime. On the first evening we were introduced to our instructor for the week, three of us to one of him. We had a fleet of Vauxhall cars, standard saloons, large and small, and 4x4 off-roaders, to one of which we were allocated in our groups of three the next morning. We spent the day taking turns at driving, improving our awareness of the road situation, and giving a running commentary as we drove through town, country and on motorways. We learned how to drive a 4x4 on a ploughed field, and attempted to park a trailer in a coned-off space, with considerable redesigning of the shape of the cones. We learned how to check oil and tyre pressure, and how to change a wheel. Some of us travelled down to Brooklands to do some skid car training, learning how to deal with icy roads, black ice and aqua-planning. The final day was devoted to our individual assessments, and I was delighted to hear that I'd passed. I have been a member of the Institute of Advanced Motorists ever since.

Elizabeth Lovesey, Spilsby WI

The Denman Derailleurs

We are the students and tutors of the first ever Bicycle Maintenance & Safe Cycling course, held at Denman in June 1993. Among our group, aged from eighteen to sixty-five, were cycle tourists, family potterers, leisurely day-riders, shopping-bikers and dedicated racing women. For three days, the dining room at Denman rang with conversation about bearings and cables, ratios and Allen keys, and oil-smeared women lined up for coffee alongside those there to learn to play bridge. We all kept in touch and held regular reunions – and in due course husbands joined us too. We were pleased to treat with sympathy their inexperience, going slowly up hills and looking for tea stops – and one must admit, they have stronger wrists when it comes to taking off a tyre. Men have their uses. **Marguerite Shaw**

'I have been a member of the WI for twenty-eight years, belonging to four different WIs around the country, and have been to Denman forty-four times so far.'

Denman has run advanced driving courses since the 1950s.

Tea break, 1960s.

My WI life of friendship goes back seventy years to when, aged twenty, I was demobbed after two years in the WRNS. It was January 1947 during one of the coldest winters when I returned to village life at Hawkesbury Upton in Gloucestershire: no electric power or piped water there, very primitive sanitation, and above all – nothing to do! Such a change from dancing in the NAAFI club and going to the cinema in Plymouth. One night, when I was having my usual moan, my mum suggested I go to the WI with her. I was not very eager, but desperation drove me to join her and I was surprised to find it was not too bad! The ladies welcomed me and treated me as if I'd won the war single-handedly, so gradually I started going to the meetings and joined. I remember that much of the discussion at the time was about finding somewhere to have a WI college. This caused a mixed reaction among some of the men of the village, but my dad was quite enlightened and agreed with it.

I am now ninety years of age and sitting here with my memories. I shed a tear for friends no longer with us and smile at funny incidents in the past. I think of all the speakers we have enjoyed and all the resolutions presented to HM Government, many of which have been incorporated into the statute books. I give my thanks to the WI for seventy years of priceless friendship. The aim of the WI was to improve the lives of women, initially in the countryside and now everywhere. So much has been achieved and there is still a long way to go but, if we continue to work together, we will get there.

Valerie Lewington, Chipping Sodbury Morning WI

I have been on several courses at Denman in my thirty-plus years of membership, each different and each very enjoyable. I chose Singing Dusty Springfield this time, in June 2017, as I wanted simply to enjoy myself for a few days of being just me. At dinner I chatted to other members and found out that there were sixteen of us singing, while others were doing oil pastel painting, cheesemaking, beading and embroidery. The College was almost full, buzzing with new friendships being made, wine being shared over dinner, and notes being compared on our journeys. On the first evening we met our lovely tutor, Jo Sercombe, and she put us straight into learning the first of Dusty's songs. Jo was an encouraging, clever, funny woman, and we had a great time throughout. We learnt three songs and sang her arrangements of them in three-part harmony, choosing to be grouped into high, middle and low voices. Sometimes we were the backing group, sometimes Dusty, and she had arranged it so that we all got a go at everything. Our singing experience varied, but there was no standard to live up to and we all felt we could sing by the end of the course, when we put on a concert for all of the other courses to come to. Several of the group signed up straightaway for another of Jo's courses next summer. We had nothing to take home like everyone else, but we had our pride and, boy, did we have fun!

Penny Noble

'The aim of the WI was to improve the lives of women, initially in the countryside and now everywhere. So much has been achieved and there is still a long way to go but, if we continue to work together, we will get there.'

Dancing, 1950s. Since its opening in 1948, and up to the present day, meeting like-minded people and having a good time with new friends has been a central part of the experience at Denman.

The stunning setting of Denman, beautifully captured here on a summer's day, offers students as much a place of respite and relaxation as it does study.

Having only been to Denman once before, to a talk, I was a bit apprehensive about spending a weekend there for the Making the Magic course in May 2017. Following the induction on the first evening, we had drinks in the bar and then dinner. The food was excellent and we had the time to meet lots of other WI members from all over the country, many of whom had been given their course as a gift for Christmas. Some elderly ladies told me that they no longer want to travel but they choose to do a course at Denman rather than go on holiday, not just because they find the experience stimulating but mostly because they feel safe at Denman. The course was fun; there were only three of us on it and we all got along really well as a group. My nervousness was unfounded and I would definitely do another course at Denman. And I can also see how important it is to save the College for the future.

Judy Siemers

In 1981 I attended a Writing for Pleasure and Profit course. I shared a very comfortable room with my friend, who was doing Patchwork. At just twenty-nine years old I was one of the youngest there, and was also one of the few pregnant women to attend Denman; my son (my third child) was born in the December of that year. I remember everyone being so friendly. It was such a treat to be enjoying real ME time, focusing purely on MY needs and interests, and having the most fantastic meals put in front of me without lifting a finger. The luxury of it! But most of all I remember the last night, when our group performed a revue. I was so proud to have penned new words to 'Land of Hope and Glory' which the others all sang. It was titled 'Girls of Denman College' and I can remember it now:

> *Girls of Denman College*
> *Lovers of the arts*
> *Home and Country readers*
> *Budding Lionel Barts*
> *Wider still and wider*
> *Must our voice be heard*
> *Go and show the nation*
> *Through your deeds and words*
> *Tell them all of Denman*
> *Go and spread the word!*

I so enjoyed those few days. I gained self-confidence and learned such a lot. Denman is definitely a unique experience.

Sallie Hammond, Atwick WI

I was just a young forty-year-old on my first visit to Denman in February 1976 and continued attending regularly for the next forty years. I have seen many changes and witnessed Denman becoming the successful establishment it is today. My first course was a cookery demonstration held in a lecture room – this was before the Home Economics Centre had been built. I still use the moussaka recipe I learnt on that course. Until 2001, I always visited on my own as I enjoyed meeting other members. But as I got older it was more convenient to join the Glamorgan Federation weekends held every eighteen months. I was so elated after my first visit in 1976 that I suggested my WI should set up a Denman bursary. This was agreed, and still continues. Other members of my WI also regularly take courses at the College, and when the Save Denman appeal was launched in 1985, Tonteg WI showed its support by contributing £1,200 raised from a Historical Fashion Show held at the City Hall in Cardiff. I like to think that, as the first person from my WI to go to Denman, I have encouraged others to enjoy that wonderful 'Denman experience'.

Mair Morgan, Tonteg WI

I have been on three courses at Denman and enjoyed them all, but perhaps the most memorable in some ways was a walking course in the upper Thames valley, because it was on the weekend of Princess Diana's funeral. There was some discussion as to whether the College would open, but the decision was taken that the courses would go ahead and the students had the choice of continuing with their course or watching the proceedings on television. I opted to walk, and just before 11am we reached a lovely copse with tall cathedral-like trees near the Thames, where the group stopped and observed a minute's silence for Diana, close to the river that was also flowing near where all those in London were doing the same. It was very moving. We walked on and arrived in Lechlade where we went to the church and signed the book of remembrance there.

Sue Farr

I'd always heard about Denman – a beautiful place with mouthwatering food – but as I lived so far away it seemed out of reach and I never thought I'd get there. In 2017 my WI offered two bursaries for a Denman visit and I never thought I'd win one, but I did! The other winner, another member and I chose the Calligraphy course in August. Denman lived up to everything I'd heard about it – the most beautiful setting, comfortable rooms, the best food ever, fantastic staff. To top it all, the course was brilliant: hard work but enjoyable, and our tutor was so good at making it a pleasure to learn and entertaining while he did it. I'd go back in a heartbeat, it was just the best time ever. Thank you Denman, I'll never forget it.

Maureen Hayes

'I like to think that, as the first person from my WI to go to Denman, I have encouraged others to enjoy that wonderful "Denman experience".'

Subscribers

Aberhonddu WI, Powys Brecknock Federation

Alison Adams

Mary Adams

Pam Adcock

Sandy Adcock, Cusgarne and Frogpool WI

Julie Alen

Christine Alexander, Milton on Stour WI

Janet Allum

Valerie Alsford

Liz Anderson

Andover Afternoon WI, Hampshire Federation

Lynne Andrews

Jennie Antliff

Colleen Arnott

Lesley Ashworth

Pamela D Austin

Julie Ayre

Elizabeth Baily

Sally Ball

Sarah Banks

Jane Bass

Fariba Battye

June Bayles

Yvonne Bee

Pam Beedan

Jan Bell

Anne Bennett

Linda Bennett

Elizabeth Berry

Janis Bethel

Patricia Louisa Betts

Fiona Birchall

Rosemary Bishton MBE

Eileen Lynne Black

Margaret Blackwell

Jennifer Blake

Paul Blake

June Blandy and Jenny Gooding

Catherine Blaxhall

Jan Blight

Lotty Boersma

Boldre WI

Maggie Bond

Pauline Bowman

Kathy Bradley and Dawn Beswick

Annette Bradshaw

Anne Brain

Bramford WI

Angela Brice

Rebe Brick

Christine Bridger

Susan Bridger

Janice Bridges

Brightwell-cum-Sotwell WI

Val Brooks

Carol M Brown

Penelope Brown

Jennifer Brunskill

Buckinghamshire Federation

Anne Bullman

Di Burgum

Madeleine Burr

Wendy Burrows

Jenny Burton, Aylsebury Town WI

Donna Butcher

Ann Carter

Helen Carter

Ceredigion Federation

Wendy Chapman

Charlesworth WI

Chelsfield Evening WI

Barbara Churchward

Mary Clarke

Pamela Clarke

Cliddesden WI

Clifton WI, Bedfordshire Federation

Rona Coates, Baldrine WI, Isle of Man Federation

Sue Cocker

Brenda Cogswell

Jane Collier

Anne Conchar

Margaret Cooke

Carol Coombs

Ros Cooper

Cotswold Duston WI

Jean Cox

Susan Crawford

Creekside WI, Wootton, Isle of Wight Federation

Maureen Crew

Croft Marsh and District WI

Maureen Crosby-Kinson

Sally Dalley

Linda Davey

Gill Davies

Mellis Davis

Norma Deane

Nellie Dearden

Katherine Dempster

Christine Denton

Denvilles WI

Jennifer Derby

Devon Federation

J Maureen Dickens

Diss WI

Dorothy Douse

Heather Duffin

Dundry WI

Pat Dunnill

Liz Eaton

Lesley Eccles

Carol Eccleston

Barbara Eddowes

Patricia Eden

Ann Edmunds

Louise Edwards

Jill Eldridge

Rachel Ellins

Jill Elliott

Joy Elliott

Veronica Elliott, Lustleigh WI

Patricia Elwell

Jean Emes

Erme WI, Ivybridge, Devon Federation

Essex Federation

Julie Evans

Lesley Evans

Hazel Everett

Sandra Fenton

Elizabeth Fisher

Rosie Fisher

Rose Fitzgerald

Emma Fleming

Ann Fletcher

Marian Forsythe

Elsie Foster

Annette Foulds

Sally Fox

Ann France

Brenda Francis

Carolyn Frank

Jill Free

Claire Gardiner

Suey Gaythorpe

Denise Gee

Barbara George

Dinah Gibbons, Bwlchllan WI

Olive Gibson

Giggleswick WI, North Yorkshire West Federation

Valerie Gill

Julie Gillett

Gillian Glover

Liz Goldie

Linda Golding
Eileen Gomme
Marion Gough
Lindsay Gow
Marion Grant
Sheila Grant
Monica Gray
Priscilla Gray
Great Missenden Evening WI
Greatstone WI
Julia Green
Rosemary Green
Sally Green
Joan Griffiths, Bridport Centre WI,
    Dorset Federation
Anne Gurr
Gwynedd Meirionnydd Federation
Alison Haigh
Jennifer Haines
Marylyn Haines-Evans
Ann Frances Hall
Kelsie Hall
Shirley Hall
Thelma Halling
Jennifer Hamel-Cooke
Rosemary Hamilton
Sue Hamilton
Patricia Hammond
Sallie Hammond
Margaret Hanley
Harbury WI
Jean Harding
Margaret Harman
Jacqueline Harris, Nightingales WI
Caroline Harrison
Anne Harvey
Emily Harvey
Susan E Harvey
Sylvia Haslett
Mary Haughton
Jackie Hawes
Hilary Hawkes
Hawkinge Evening WI
Margaret Hawkins
Hawley WI

Pat Heath
Teresa Hemms
Christine Anne Hemsley
Elaine Henshaw
Linda Hewett
Hewish and District WI
Mary Hewitt
Highweek WI
Highworth Evening WI
Barbara Hill
Jacquie Hillard
Valerie J Hillier
Anne Hingley
Maureen Hipkiss
Susanne Hoadley
Mary Hoban, East Barkwith and
    District WI
Joan Hodgkinson and Sheila Allsopp
Pauline Holbrook
Deidre Holes
Poppy Hollins-Gibson
Jane Holmes
Jean Holmes
Helen Hooley
Kay Hopkinson
Christine Hounslow
Ingrid House
Kim Howard
Margaret E A Hughes
Sheila M Hughes
Sally Hulme
Eileen Hurd
Frances Hurndall
Sharon Hurrell
Anne Hutt
Carole Hyde-Smith
Sylvia Insley
Valerie Irving
Angie Ison
Valerie Jackson
Vivienne James
June Jamieson-Peskett
Pauline Janikoun
Kate Jeeps
Doreen Jeeves

Jane Jefferson
Connie Jeffery
Lorna Jenkins
Valerie Joyce Jenner
Jinny Jerome
Ann Jones
Betty Jones
Hazel Jones
Jennifer Jones and Patricia Billington
Yvonne Jordan
Beyrl Jull
Catherine Keeling
Josephine Kemp
Lyn Kendal-Archer
Sue Kendall
Debbie Kennedy
Kennington WI
Amanda Key
Anne Kiltie
Sandra Kinchin
Jeanie King
Shirley King
Kingswood WI, Avon Federation
Kirby Muxloe WI
Lynda Kiss
Lambourn WI
Kathy Lane
Janice Langley
Peter Lawrence
Virginia Lawrence
Christina Lee
Susan Leicester
Leigh WI
Valerie Lewington
Ann Lewis
Patricia Lewis
Irene Lindsay
Little Gaddesden WI
Little Marlow and Well End WI
Theresa Lloyd
Lovedean WI
Gill Loveluck
Elizabeth Lovesey
Jim Lowden
Lustleigh WI

Lynsted with Teynham WI
Ann Maasz
Sally Mabey
Muriel Macmaster
June Maidens
Judi Marie
Lorraine Markham
Gillian Marks, Aylesbury Town WI
Penny Marsh
Jacqueline Marshall-Llewellyn
Susan Marshfield
Sarah Mascall
Dorothy Maskell MBE
Judith Massey
Jayne Maxwell
Sue Maylam
Sandra McArdle
Sheena McDonald
Sue McNaughton
Pauline McQuistan
Jennifer Melotte
Messingham WI, Lincolnshire
    North Federation
Margaret Mills
Misterton WI
Emma Jane Monaghan
Beryl Moore
Mair Morgan, Tonteg WI,
    Glamorgan Federation
Joy Morgan
Susan A Morgan
Audrey Morrison
Angela Mottram
Claire Muir
Margaret F Mundy
Pauline Murphy
Susan Murphy
Pam Myers
Susan Neale
Paula Neall
Connie Newman
Shirley Newman
Patricia Newsham
Linda Nicholls
Gillian Nokes

Helen Nutbeam

Linda Odell

Kathryn M Ogden

Ruth Oliver

Edna Oswald

Sandra Overton

Dorothy Padgham

Jean Page

Carys Palmer

Shirley Parkin

June Parrett

Colette Parsons

Elizabeth Patterson

Christina Paul

Jenny Pearson

Judith Penneck

Jean Penny

Eireen Perkins

Joan Perry

Patricia Peters

Ann Phythian

Paula Pierce

Glynis Pilbeam

Margaret Pilkington

Pinchbeck WI

Janet Pinches

Doreen Pinnell

Sarah Plumley

Patricia Pratley

Prestbury WI

Barbara Prime

Mary Prior

Jane Probitts

Pumsaint WI

Cate Purcell

Jinty Pyke

Linda Rachel

Tina Raddenbury

Radley WI

Barbara Ramshaw

Ravenstone and Snibston WI

Redlands WI, Berkshire Federation

Lorraine Reed-Wenman

Joan Ricketts

Valerie Ridgman

Iris Rigg

Arlene Riley

Ringmer Evening WI,
    East Sussex Federation

Tracy-lee Rogers

Ann Romain

Royston Afternoon WI

Ruskington WI

Deborah Sanders

Stewart Saulter

Ann Savill

Penny Savill

Diane Sawyer

Franzeska Sawyer,
    Aylsebury Town WI

Joyce Schaffer

Jean Scott

Rosalind Seall

Jane Sealy

Anne Seckington

Caroline Selby

Vivienne Selier

Linda Sellers

Shirley Seymour

Lynda Sharpe

Shedfield WI

Mary Sheldon

Joan Sherrin

Anne Short, Andover
    Afternoon WI

Pat Shotton

Margaret Simcock

Sue Simpson

Kate Skinner

Carole Smith

Georgina (Gina) Mary Moncreiff
    Smith

Heather Smith

Maureen Smith

Shirley Smith

St Buryan WI

St Day WI

Anne Stamper

Jean Stanbury

Rosemary Stark, Ashtead WI

Frankie Stephens

Cathrine Stone

Jeryl Stone

Heather Joan Stopps

Carolyn Stroud

Lynne Stubbings

Dianne Surgey

Angela Sutherland

Sutton Courtenay WI

Veronica Taunt

Edith Taylor

Helen Taylor

Joy Taylor

Joyce Thacker

Sue Thomas

Ellen Mary Thompson

Kate Thorlby-Coy

Bridget Thurgood

Mavis Thurgood

Tibberton and Taynton WI

Tilehurst Afternoon WI

Miriam Tilt

Liz Tipping

Todmorden WI

Towcester Evening WI

Christine Toynton, Yaxley WI

Dorothy Tozer

Pat Trede

Jill Treeves

Jane Treharne

Patricia Tulip

Valerie Tull

Frances Unsworth

Vale WI, Guernsey Federation

Judy Venn

Wadsworth WI

Sally Wakefield

Sandra Walker

Barbara Wallis

Florence Walsh

Valerie Walsh

Sandra Walters

Sonia Warby

Angie Ward

Jenny Ward

Muriel Wardle, Old Brampton WI

Waterford WI, Hertfordshire
    Federation

Vicky Watkins

Jan Watson

Elizabeth A Watt

Sheila Webber

Elizabeth Webster

Judith Weeks

Niobe A Wells

Lesley West

Irene Weston

Whissendine WI

Frances Whitaker, Cropredy WI

Whitchurch Hill WI

Eileen White

Gail Whitehurst

Yolande Whitley

Ann Whittaker

Patricia Ann Wilcox

Angie Williams

Ann Williams, Little Gaddesden WI

Jane Williams

Judy Williamson

Jillian Willson, Hauxton WI

Kathleen Wilson, Isle of Man
    Federation

Sue Wilson

Ruth Winch

Windsor Great Park WI

Margaret A S Winterbourne

Barbara Wiseman

Shirley Wood

Elizabeth Woodall,
    Clee St Margaret WI

Jackie Woolsey

Carole Wright, Emsworth
    Morning WI

Muriel (Becky) Wright

Wyke Regis WI

Gillian Yarham

Karen Yates

M J Yetton

Author's Acknowledgements

This book would have been considerably more difficult to produce without the hugely generous help of Anne Stamper, Denman archivist and author of *Rooms Off the Corridor: Education in the WI and Fifty Years of Denman College 1948–1998* (WI Books, 1998). Not only did she allow me to make full use of the extensive research in her book, but she was often on hand at Denman to guide me through the archives and put me right when I got things wrong. I am massively grateful to her. Another useful resource was Barbara Kaye's *Live and Learn: The Story of Denman College 1948–1969* (NFWI, 1970), published for the College's twenty-first birthday. And the Denman archives were full of memories, anecdotes, facts and figures about the developing institution, as well as plenty of images, some of them published here for the first time.

My research at the College was underpinned and eased by the welcome and help I enjoyed from the staff – particularly Jane Dixon and Ruba Asfahani – as well as the students with whom I discussed their experiences of Denman and of WI membership. I quickly learned that the College has open arms and fantastic warmth!

Right Peter Lawrence, a long-standing history and heritage tutor, presented this postcard to the archives, signed on the back by all the students on one of his courses in the 1960s.

About the author

Val Horsler graduated in classics and then, for over thirty years, pursued a career in archaeological publishing, latterly at English Heritage. She now concentrates on writing and editing, and has published a range of books for the National Archives and Third Millennium, for whom she has written celebrations of Holy Trinity Church Stratford, the Order of Malta, the Inner Temple and the Cavalry and Guards Club, among many others. She is also the author of *Women's Century*, commissioned by the WI to celebrate its centenary in 2015.

THE DENMAN COLLEGE. MARCHAM PARK. ABINGDON

Picture credits

The majority of the archive images are from either the Denman College archive or the WI Archive at the Women's Library of the London School of Economics.

Other sources are listed below. Every effort has been made to contact the copyright holders of the images featured in the book. In the case of an inadvertent omission, please contact the publisher.

© NFWI/WIE and Third Millennium Publishing, 2018

First published in 2018 by Third Millennium Publishing, an imprint of Profile Books Ltd

3 Holford Yard
Bevin Way
London
United Kingdom
WC1X 9HD
www.tmbooks.com

ISBN 978 1 78816 017 9

Editing: Val Horsler
Design: Caroline Clark
Production: Simon Shelmerdine
Reprograhics by BORN London
Printed and bound in China by 1010 International Ltd on acid-free paper from sustainable forestry